How to Use this Book

Matched to the National Curriculum, this Collins Year 5 Comprehension workbook is designed to improve compr... ...skills.

Diverse and engaging texts including **fiction**, **non-fiction** and **poetry**.

Tests **increase in difficulty** as you work through the book.

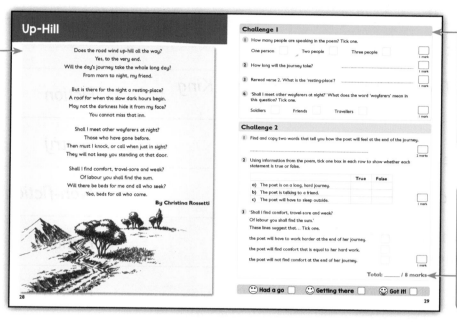

Questions split into three levels of difficulty – **Challenge 1**, **Challenge 2** and **Challenge 3** – to help progression.

Total marks boxes for recording progress and '**How am I doing**' checks for self-evaluation.

Starter test recaps skills covered in Year 4.

Three **Progress tests** included throughout the book for ongoing assessment and monitoring progress.

Starter Test

Extract from

Kidnapped! The Hundred-Mile-an-Hour Dog's Sizzling Summer
by Jeremy Strong

Chapter 1: Jabbed with the Eiffel Tower

You can't blame me. All I did was jump out of the window. OK, so it was the big window at the vet's surgery. Mrs Vet-Person shouldn't have left it open, should she, and anyhow, what would you do if a vet came at you with a whopping great big needle?

'Just a tiny jab,' Mrs Vet-Person said. Oh yes! I saw the evil grin on her face AND I saw the size of the pointy needle. Big? It looked like the Eiffel Tower! I was off like a streak of lightning. (No, actually, I was off like a Streaker because that is my name – Streaker – and I am the speediest speedster in the World of Dog-Speed.)

I saw the vet, I saw the needle and I saw the open window. *SWOOOOOSH!* I was gone in a flish-flash! Ha ha! You can stick that needle in someone else's bottom, Mrs Vet-Person!

They all came chasing after me of course, but I was way too fast for them. Those two-legs can't run properly at all. I keep barking at them. 'Use all four legs! You can't run properly on two! You've got to use all four legs, like me!' But they never hear. That's because they have very small ears, unlike mine, which go flip-flap like towels on a washing line. I can catch the teeny-tiniest sounds, even like an ant sneezing or an earwig with earache going 'Ooooh!' in a very small earwiggy voice like that.

Of course I was in big trouble at home after I'd run away from Mrs Vet-Person. Even Trevor Two-Legs, the boy I have to take for walks, was fed up. I thought he'd be pleased at my nifty bit of escapery but he wasn't. He was upset.

'It's for your own good, Streaker,' he told me.

Oh, really? My own good? I don't think so! I said, 'I'd like to see you get vaccinated with the Eiffel Tower!' Of course he didn't understand a word I said. Humans are hopeless. What's the point in having a dog as a pet if you can't understand what it tells you?

6

Progress Test 3

8. Why did Scrooge keep the door of his counting-house open?
    _____ 1 mark

9. '...in a dismal little cell beyond, a sort of tank...' What impression do you get of the room where the clerk worked? Give two impressions.
    a) _____
    b) _____ 2 marks

10. 'But he couldn't replenish it...' Who or what does 'he' refer to in this sentence?
    _____ 1 mark

11. How did the clerk try to keep warm? Find two things.
    a) _____
    b) _____ 2 marks

12. '"Bah!" said Scrooge. "Humbug!"' What does 'humbug' mean? Tick one.
    Nonsense ☐   Perhaps ☐   Correct ☐ 1 mark

13. 'What right have you to be dismal?' Find another place where the writer uses the word 'dismal' to describe something. What was it?
    _____ 1 mark

14. 'What reason have you to be morose?' 'Morose' means... Tick one.
    cold. ☐   gloomy. ☐   cheerful. ☐ 1 mark

15. What impressions do you get of Scrooge's nephew? Give one impression, supporting your answer with evidence from the text.
    _____
    _____ 2 marks

88

Answers provided for all the questions.

Contents

Acknowledgments

The author and publisher are grateful to the copyright holders for permission to use quoted materials and images.

Permission to print City Jungle by Pie Corbett. Copyright of Pie Corbett http://www.talk4writing.com/; THE IRON GIANT by Ted Hughes, text copyright © 1968 by Ted Hughes, copyright renewed 1996 by Ted Hughes. Used by permission of Alfred A. Knopf, an imprint of Random House Children's Books, a division of Penguin Random House LLC. All rights reserved. The Iron Man by Ted Hughes also used by permission of Faber and Faber Ltd; "Dirty Face" from Every Thing On It by Shel Silverstein illustrated by: Shel Silverstein. Used by permission of HarperCollins Publishers; 'Timothy Winters' from *Collected Poems for Children* by Charles Causley (Macmillan Children's Books), reproduced by permission by David Higham Associates; 'The Quarrel' by Eleanor Farjeon reproduced by permission by David Higham Associates; 'Coming to England' by Floella Benjamin ©Copyright, Floella Benjamin 2020. Published by Macmillan, is used by permission; Journey to Jo'burg reprinted by permission of HarperCollins Publishers Ltd © 2008 Beverley Naidoo; '*Kidnapped! The Hundred-Mile-an-Hour Dog's Sizzling Summer*' by Jeremy Strong © 2014, was published by Puffin; 'A Smile' taken from Shake Before Opening, by Spike Milligan; 'The Lion and the Unicorn' by Shirley Hughes, published by Random House © Shirley Hughes 1998; 'Hacker' by Malorie Blackman, published by Random House, UK. © Copyright Malorie Blackman, 1992; 'Jumbo Jet' was taken from: Silly Verse for Kids by Spike Milligan, published by Puffin. © Copyright, Spike Milligan, 2015; 'All About Canals' was found at the Canal & Rivers Trust https://canalrivertrust.org.uk/media/library/31148.pdf

All illustrations and images are ©Shutterstock.com and ©HarperCollins Publishers Ltd.

Published by Collins
An imprint of HarperCollins*Publishers*
1 London Bridge Street
London SE1 9GF

HarperCollins*Publishers*
Macken House, 39/40 Mayor Street Upper,
Dublin 1, D01 C9W8, Ireland

© HarperCollins*Publishers* Limited 2021

ISBN 978-0-00-846759-3

First published 2021

10 9 8 7 6 5 4 3

All rights reserved. No part of this publication may be reproduced, stored in a retrieval system, or transmitted, in any form or by any means, electronic, mechanical, photocopying, recording or otherwise, without the prior permission of Collins.

British Library Cataloguing in Publication Data.

A CIP record of this book is available from the British Library.

Publisher: Fiona McGlade
Author: Rachel Grant
Copyeditor: Fiona Watson
Project Management: Shelley Teasdale
Cover Design: Sarah Duxbury
Inside Concept Design and Page Layout: Ian Wrigley
Production: Karen Nulty
Printed and bound in the United Kingdom

FSC — MIX — Paper | Supporting responsible forestry — FSC™ C007454 — www.fsc.org

Reading Comprehension at Home

These activities can be easily carried out at home when reading for pleasure with your child, or when your child is reading for pleasure on their own. They will help build your child's comprehension skills and are fun to do.

Open questions

Help your child to develop an understanding of ideas in the texts they read. Use open questions like, 'Why did the character say that?', 'Why did the writer choose that word?' or 'What makes you think that?'. This will develop higher-order reading skills of inference and deduction and encourage children to move beyond simply decoding words.

What happens next?

When you are reading a story or narrative poem with your child, stop at a suitable point in the story and ask them to predict what will happen next, and to explain why they think that. Encourage them to think about how their understanding of the characters and the events so far helped them with their prediction.

Word families

When you are reading with your child, take the time to explore the meaning of unfamiliar words to ensure they understand what they have read. Encourage them to use the context to help them work out what new words mean, and to use a dictionary to double-check the meaning. Make a note of familiar words that have similar meanings to develop their understanding.

Picture perfect

When you are reading non-fiction with your child, consider the pictures, diagrams and charts that have been included, as well as the words. Discuss why you think those particular pictures, diagrams and charts were chosen, and how they help the reader to understand the text. Ask them to suggest other artwork they would like to see included on the page.

Reading with older children

As your child gets older, he or she may prefer silent reading on their own rather than being read to. At this point it is important to create an environment that values reading as an experience and that also fosters discussing ideas and opinions about the books you and your child are reading.

Make connections

When you are reading with your child, encourage them to make connections between the book and their own experiences. For example, you may want to ask them if they remember a time when they had a similar experience to a character in the book; if they can think of other poems with similar characters, settings or themes; or if they've seen or heard about the information you read in a non-fiction book.

Join the library

Borrowing books from your local library is an easy and inexpensive way to ensure that your child experiences a wide range of books. Children's librarians are experts at ensuring their collections are full of well-loved classics, new releases, comics, audio stories and interesting non-fiction. Many local libraries also run story sessions and arrange activity sessions aimed at encouraging reading.

Words in focus

Give your child time to work on words they find difficult to read. Don't be too quick to read it for them, but show them strategies they could use, for example breaking it down into syllables. Make sure your child understands the meaning of the word before moving on.

Extract from

Kidnapped! The Hundred-Mile-an-Hour Dog's Sizzling Summer
by Jeremy Strong

Chapter 1: Jabbed with the Eiffel Tower

You can't blame me. All I did was jump out of the window. OK, so it was the big window at the vet's surgery. Mrs Vet-Person shouldn't have left it open, should she, and anyhow, what would you do if a vet came at you with a whopping great big needle?

'Just a tiny jab,' Mrs Vet-Person said. Oh yes? I saw the evil grin on her face AND I saw the size of the pointy needle. Big? It looked like the Eiffel Tower! I was off like a streak of lightning. (No, actually, I was off like a Streaker because that is my name – Streaker – and I am the speediest speedster in the World of Dog-Speed.)

I saw the vet, I saw the needle and I saw the open window. *SWOOOOOOSH!* I was gone in a flish-flash! Ha ha! You can stick that needle in someone else's bottom, Mrs Vet-Person!

They all came chasing after me of course, but I was way too fast for them. Those two-legs can't run properly at all. I keep barking at them. 'Use all four legs! You can't run properly on two! You've got to use all four legs, like me!' But they never hear. That's because they have very small ears, unlike mine, which go flip-flap like towels on a washing line. I can catch the teeny-tiniest sounds, even like an ant sneezing or an earwig with earache going 'Ooooh!' in a very small earwiggy voice like that.

Of course I was in big trouble at home after I'd run away from Mrs Vet-Person. Even Trevor Two-Legs, the boy I have to take for walks, was fed up. I thought he'd be pleased at my nifty bit of escapery but he wasn't. He was upset.

'It's for your own good, Streaker,' he told me.

Oh, really? My own good? I don't think so! I said, 'I'd like to see you get vaccinated with the Eiffel Tower!' Of course he didn't understand a word I said. Humans are hopeless. What's the point in having a dog as a pet if you can't understand what it tells you?

1. **Reread the first paragraph. What did the dog do when she was at the vet's? Tick one.**

Had a vaccination ☐

Jumped out of the window ☑

Bit the vet ☐

1 mark

2. **'...a whopping great big needle?' What does the word 'whopping' mean in this sentence? Tick one.**

Sharp ☐

Scary ☐

Extremely ☑

1 mark

3. **To the dog, the needle looked like... Find and copy a group of words to complete the sentence.**

It looked like the Eiffel Tower. ✓

1 mark

4. **'I was off like a streak of lightning.' This means that Streaker moved... Tick one.**

very quietly. ☐

very quickly. ☑

very clumsily. ☐

1 mark

5. **Using information from the text, tick one box in each row to show whether each statement is true or false.**

		True	False
a)	Streaker runs faster than humans because she uses four legs.	✓	~~✗~~
b)	Streaker can hear more than humans because she has larger ears.	✓	
c)	Humans can understand everything Streaker says.		✓

1 mark

7

6. Who did Streaker blame for the fact that she jumped out of the window?
    Tick one.

    Herself   ☐

    The reader   ☐

    The vet   ☑ ✓

7. Where was the vet going to stick the needle?

    She was going to stick it in his bottom.   ✓

8. What name does Streaker use instead of the word 'humans'? Write the name she uses.

    Two Legs.   ✓

9. 'I thought he'd be pleased at my nifty bit of escapery but he wasn't.'
    What does Striker mean by the word 'escapery' in this sentence?
    Tick one.

    Being brave   ☐

    Being able to get away ☑ ✓

    Being able to run fast ☐

10. Trevor Two-Legs said: 'It's for your own good, Streaker'. Explain why he said this.

    He is trying to encourage streaker to take the vaccine and he's also trying to tell him it's for his health. ✓

The Future of Space Travel

After months of preparation, SpaceX has announced that it has a new spaceship called *Starship*. Elon Musk, who is in charge of SpaceX, spoke from the company's headquarters in California. He said he is 'highly confident' that, with *Starship*'s new technology, SpaceX will land humans on Mars by 2026 – or even earlier 'if we get lucky'.

Starship is a vehicle with two parts that can be used over and over again. The spacecraft part is called *Starship*. The rocket part is called Super Heavy. Together they are called the Starship system. This means that *Starship* is the world's first fully reusable spaceship. SpaceX intends to replace all its existing rockets with the Starship system in the early 2020s.

SpaceX plans to send people to the Moon and to Mars. Eventually, it hopes to build bases on the planets, so that people can live there. However, this is still far off. Many test flights will need to be completed to make sure that *Starship* can launch and land safely.

Only 12 human beings have walked on the Moon so far. The first were Neil Armstrong and Edwin 'Buzz' Aldrin in 1968. The last person to walk on the Moon was Eugene Cernan in 1972. In 1971, the space probe *Mars 3* successfully landed on Mars but it stopped working 110 seconds after it landed. To date, no human being has ever landed on Mars.

Elon Musk has great ambitions for SpaceX, which he founded in 2002. He hopes that by 2035 at the latest, there will be thousands of rockets flying a million people to Mars. He knows there will be many challenges ahead but has also said, 'When something is important enough, you do it even if the odds are not in your favour.'

11. **What is the new spaceship called? Tick one.**

Super Heavy ☐

SpaceX ☐

Starship ☑

1 mark

12. **Where is the headquarters of SpaceX located?** ~~California~~

It is located in California

1 mark

13. **Look at paragraph 2. Find and copy one word that means 'can be used over and over again'.**

~~Reault~~ The word is 'reusable'.

1 mark

14. **Using information from the text, tick one box in each row to show whether each statement is true or false.**

		True	False
a)	More than 12 human beings have walked on the Moon so far.		✓
b)	The Starship system has two parts.	✓	
c)	Elon Musk founded SpaceX.	✓	

1 mark

15. **Which two planets does SpaceX plan to send people to?**

The two planets are the ^Moon and Mars.

2 marks

10

16. Look at the last paragraph. Find and copy a word that shows that flying a million people to Mars will not be easy.

The word is 'challenges'.

1 mark

17. Number these events about space exploration from 1 to 5 to show the order in which they happened. The first one has been done for you.

Mars 3 landed on Mars.	2
SpaceX was founded.	4
Eugene Cernan walked on the Moon.	3
Starship was announced by SpaceX.	5
'Buzz' Aldrin walked on the Moon.	1

1 mark

18. Why does SpaceX hope to build bases on the planets?

They hope to build bases on the planet so people can live there.

1 mark

19. What does Elon Musk hope that SpaceX will do by 2026?

He hopes that ~~he'll~~ SpaceX will land humans on Mars in 2026.

1 mark

20. '…the odds are not in your favour.' When Elon Musk says this, he means that… Tick one.

it will probably be successful. ☐

it will probably not be successful. ✓

other people think that it is an odd thing to do. ☐

1 mark

A Smile

Smiling is infectious,
you catch it like the flu.
When someone smiled at me today
I started smiling, too.

I passed around the corner
and someone saw my grin.
When he smiled, I realised,
I'd passed it on to him.

I thought about my smile and then
I realised its worth.
A single smile like mine could travel
right around the earth.

If you feel a smile begin
don't leave it undetected.
Let's start an epidemic quick
and get the world infected.

By Jez Alborough

21. In verse 1, what does the poet say smiling is like?

....

22. According to verse 1, 'Smiling is infectious'. 'Infectious' means that smiling... Tick one.

can be passed from one person to another. ☐

is hard to do. ☐

makes you feel happy. ☐

23. In verse 3, what does the poet realise about his smile?

....

24. In the last verse, what advice does the poet give? Tick one.

If you feel like smiling, do it. ☐

If you feel like smiling, don't do it. ☐

Do not smile at anyone. ☐

25. According to the poem, how could a single smile travel right around the world?

....

....

Total: _____ / 26 marks

Aesop's Fable: The Frogs who Wished for a King

Aesop was a slave and a storyteller who lived in Ancient Greece. This is one of the many fables he wrote.

The Frogs were tired of ruling themselves.

They had so much freedom that it had spoiled them. All day, they did nothing but sit by the pond, croaking in a bored way. They wished for a ruler who could entertain them with the pomp and display of royalty, and rule them in a way that would make them know they were being ruled.

The Frogs had a meeting and decided to send a letter to Jupiter, asking him to give them a king.

Jupiter saw what simple and foolish creatures the Frogs were. To make them think they had a king, he threw down a huge log, which fell into the water with a great splash.

At first, the Frogs hid themselves among the reeds and grasses, thinking the new king to be some fearful giant. However, they soon discovered how tame and peaceable King Log was.

The younger Frogs used him for a diving platform. The older Frogs used him for a meeting place, and soon they were complaining again to Jupiter about the king he had sent them.

Jupiter decided to teach the Frogs a lesson. He sent a Crane to be king of Frogland. King Crane was a very different sort of king from old King Log. He began to gobble up the poor Frogs and they soon saw what fools they had been. In mournful croaks, they begged Jupiter to take away cruel King Crane.

'What?' cried Jupiter. 'Are you not yet content? You have what you asked for and so you have only yourselves to blame for your misfortunes.'

Moral: Be sure you can improve your situation before you seek to change it.

Challenge 1

1 What were the Frogs tired of? ....

☐ 1 mark

2 The Frogs wished for... Tick one.

a log. ☐ a crane. ☐ a ruler. ☐

☐ 1 mark

3 Find and copy two words that tell you what Jupiter thought about the Frogs.

....

☐ 2 marks

4 What did Jupiter first send the Frogs? ....

☐ 1 mark

Challenge 2

1 What did the Frogs think of King Log? Tick one.

They thought he was boring. ☐

They thought he was powerful. ☐

They thought he was interesting. ☐

☐ 1 mark

2 How did Jupiter teach the Frogs a lesson?

....

☐ 1 mark

3 'In mournful croaks, they begged Jupiter to take away cruel King Crane.' Which word is closest in meaning to 'mournful'? Tick one.

Angry ☐ Happy ☐ Sad ☐

☐ 1 mark

4 Using information from the text, tick one box in each row to show whether each statement is true or false.

		True	False
a)	Jupiter knew the Frogs would not like King Crane.		
b)	The Frogs did not realise they had been foolish.		
c)	The moral of the story is that change is always good.		

☐ 1 mark

Total: _____ / 9 marks

😐 **Had a go** ☐   🙂 **Getting there** ☐   😄 **Got it!** ☐

The Quarrel

I quarrelled with my brother,

I don't know what about,

One thing led to another

And somehow we fell out.

The start of it was slight,

The end of it was strong,

He said he was right,

I knew he was wrong!

We hated one another.

The afternoon turned black.

Then suddenly my brother

Thumped me on the back,

And said, 'Oh, come on!

We can't go on all night—

I was in the wrong.'

So he was in the right.

By Eleanor Farjeon

Challenge 1

1. 'One thing led to another...' This shows that the quarrel was... Tick one.

   important. ☐

   planned. ☐

   accidental. ☐

   ☐ 1 mark

2. 'And somehow we fell out.' What does 'fell out' mean? Tick one.

   Tripped ☐

   Quarrelled ☐

   Made friends ☐

   ☐ 1 mark

3. How did they feel about one another when they quarrelled?

   ....

   ☐ 1 mark

Challenge 2

1. 'The afternoon turned black.' The poet says this because she felt... Tick one.

   pleased. ☐   excited. ☐   upset. ☐

   ☐ 1 mark

2. Who ended the quarrel? ....

   ☐ 1 mark

3. The brother said he made a mistake. Copy the words he said that tell you this.

   ....

   ☐ 1 mark

4. 'So he was in the right.' Explain why the poet said her brother was 'in the right'.

   ....

   ....

   ....

   ☐ 1 mark

   Total: _____ / 7 marks

Recipe for French Toast

It may surprise you to know that French Toast probably didn't come from France.

Some say we can trace the recipe back to Roman times. Others say it was created by cooks in Medieval England.

It has several other names, including German Toast, Eggy Bread, French Fried Bread and Nun's Toast, to name a few.

In France, it is called 'pain perdu' which means 'lost bread'. This tells us that it was a way of using up stale bread. Dipping the stale slices in liquid makes the bread soft again, and pleasant to eat. This means the bread is not wasted. (You don't have to use stale bread, though. Fresh bread is fine!)

No matter who created it, or what you choose to call it, almost everyone agrees that French Toast is delicious.

Difficulty level: Easy
Time: 5 minutes preparation + 10 minutes cooking
Serves: 2

Ingredients

- 3 eggs
- 2 tbsp of milk
- Sugar (optional)
- 4 slices of bread
- Butter, for frying

Equipment

- A bowl, big enough to fit a slice of bread
- A fork or a whisk
- A plate
- A frying pan

Method

1. Crack the eggs into the bowl.
2. Add the milk. If you want to make sweet French Toast, add sugar to taste.
3. Whisk the mixture. You can use a fork or a whisk for this.
4. Dip one slice of bread in the egg mixture. Coat both sides and place on a plate.
5. Repeat with the other slices of bread.
6. Heat a little butter in a frying pan and fry the bread slices one by one for 2–3 minutes on each side.

Serving suggestions

French Toast is delicious on its own, but you can add almost any kind of topping you like.

Savoury options: top with bacon or cheese.

Sweet options: top with honey, syrup, bananas, berries, or chocolate sauce.

Challenge 1

1 Find and copy two other names for French Toast.

_____

2 'Pain perdu' is French for... Tick one.

plain bread. ☐   lost bread. ☐   stale bread. ☐

☐

3 Using information from the text, tick one box in each row to show whether each statement is true or false.

		True	False
a)	French Toast probably comes from France.		
b)	French Toast is a good way of using up stale bread.		
c)	French Toast is good to eat on its own.		
d)	You cannot make French Toast without sugar.		

☐

4 How much time do you need to make French Toast? Tick one.

5 minutes ☐   10 minutes ☐   15 minutes ☐

☐

Challenge 2

1 Draw lines to match each heading to its purpose.

Ingredients   Tools you need
Equipment   What you need to do
Method   Food items you need

☐

2 You want to make sweet French Toast. Find and copy two words that tell you

how much sugar to add. _____

☐

3 'Whisk the mixture.' Which word is closest in meaning to 'whisk'? Tick one.

Sweep ☐   Whip ☐   Combine ☐

☐

4 Which section of the recipe gives the reader some ideas for making French Toast

even more delicious? _____

☐

Total: _____ / 9 marks

☺☺ **Had a go** ☐   ☺ **Getting there** ☐   ☺ **Got it!** ☐

The Lion and the Unicorn

Lenny and his mum lived during the Blitz of World War II, when German planes dropped bombs on British cities, usually at night.

'London's burning,
London's burning!
Fetch the engines,
Fetch the engines!
Fire, fire! Fire, fire!
Pour on water,
pour on water!'

Every evening, soon after dark, the warning sirens wailed. Then came the awful droning of enemy aircraft overhead, and firebombs and explosives whined and whistled out of the sky.

Lenny Levi and his mum huddled together under the stairs. Lenny clutched the badge that his dad had given him before he went away. It was made of solid brass; a lion and a unicorn up on their hind legs, fighting each other. Lenny kept it in his pocket always where he could feel it.

Dad was fighting too. He was in the army far away while Lenny and Mum clung to one another and longed for daylight.

A unicorn was a mythical beast, Dad had told him. A mysterious, gentle creature. But lions were real, all right.

Lions stood for being brave. Everybody had to be brave in wartime, not only soldiers but other people too. Children even. 'Be a brave boy, Lenny,' Dad had told him when they said goodbye.

Sometimes they got letters from Dad. They came in batches, two or three at a time. Those were the best days. Mum read bits out to Lenny while he was having his tea. Dad always put in a drawing for him. Sometimes it was a funny picture like the one of Sergeant. Once he did a beautiful picture of a unicorn with flowers around its neck.

One night the bangs shook the house so badly that they thought the roof would fall in. 'We should have gone to the shelter,' muttered Mum.

Next morning, when they went out, the Robinsons' house wasn't there any more. Their things were lying all over the street amongst the rubble and broken glass. The neighbours said that the Robinsons had gone to the Rest Centre in the night, wearing blankets.

'That's it!' said Mum. 'We've got to get you out of here, Lenny.'

By Shirley Hughes

Challenge 1

1 Which city did Lenny and his mum live in? ....
1 mark

2 'Lenny Levi and his mum huddled together under the stairs.' Why were they huddled together? Tick one.

They were cold ☐   They were scared ☐   They were calm ☐
1 mark

3 Find and copy a group of words that tells us where Lenny's dad is.

....
1 mark

4 Find and copy one word in the text that means the same as 'not real'. ....
1 mark

5 Which of these words means the same as 'creature'? Tick one.

Lion ☐   Beast ☐   Unicorn ☐
1 mark

Challenge 2

1 Using information from the text, tick one box in each row to show whether each statement is true or false.

		True	False
a)	Lions are real.		
b)	Unicorns are brave.		
c)	Lions are mysterious.		

1 mark

2 Look at the paragraph that begins 'Sometimes they got letters from Dad.' How does Lenny know that his dad is thinking about him?

....
1 mark

3 'They came in batches, two or three at a time.' Why do you think the letters came in batches of two or three?

....
1 mark

4 What has happened to the Robinsons' house? Give one piece of evidence to support your answer.

....

....
2 marks

Total: _____ / 10 marks

😐 **Had a go** ☐   🙂 **Getting there** ☐   😄 **Got it!** ☐

Dirty Face

Where did you get such a dirty face,

My darling dirty-faced child?

I got it from crawling along in the dirt

And biting two buttons off Jeremy's shirt.

I got it from chewing the roots of a rose

And digging for clams in the yard with my nose.

I got it from peeking into a dark cave

And painting myself like a Navajo brave.

I got it from playing with coal in the bin

And signing my name in cement with my chin.

I got it from rolling around on the rug

And giving the horrible dog a big hug.

I got it from finding a lost silver mine

And eating sweet blackberries right off the vine.

I got it from ice cream and wrestling and tears

And from having more fun than you've had in years.

By Shel Silverstein

Challenge 1

1 Find and copy one word from the first two lines that shows that the child is very

dear to the adult. _____

[ ] 1 mark

2 According to the poem, where did the child crawl? Tick one.

In a cave [ ] In the dirt [ ] On the rug [ ]

[ ] 1 mark

3 What did the child play with in the bin? _____

[ ] 1 mark

4 Using information from the poem, draw lines to match each activity that the child did.
The first one has been done for you.

Biting   the roots of a rose

Rolling   a lost silver mine

Chewing →   for clams in the yard

Digging   around on the rug

Finding   buttons off a shirt

[ ] 1 mark

Challenge 2

1 'And painting myself like a Navajo brave.' Which of the following words is closest in
meaning to the word *brave*? Tick one.

Warrior [ ]

King [ ]

Slave [ ]

[ ] 1 mark

2 Find and copy two foods that the child ate.

....

[ ] 2 marks

3 'And from having more fun than you've had in years.' What does this suggest that
the child thinks about the adult?

....

[ ] 1 mark

Total: _____ / 8 marks

😐 **Had a go** [ ]   🙂 **Getting there** [ ]   😄 **Got it!** [ ]

Weird News This Week

Poop Power! Honeybees find a new way to scare off hornets

New scientific study shows how honeybees defend themselves

The Asian Giant Hornet is the largest hornet species in the world. It is sometimes called the 'murder hornet' because it can attack honeybee hives. The hornets cut off the heads of the bees and use younger bees for food.

But one bee species in Vietnam has found a way of fighting back. These honeybees, called *Apis cerana* or Asian honeybee, collect small bits of animal poop and stick it near the entrance to the hive. The stinkier the poop, the better.

Bees are usually clean creatures, according to scientists. So why were these bees using poop at the mouth of their hives? The answer, the study concludes, is that the poop deters the hornets. It is thought that the stinky smell drives them away. Furthermore, the hornets usually have to chew on the hive to get into it and attack the bees. However, if the hive entrance is covered with poop, hornets are 94% less likely to chew on it, the study found.

Scientists studied more than 300 giant hornet attacks on the beehives. They concluded that more poop resulted in fewer attacks. So, using poop is a very effective way for honeybees to keep themselves safe from this predator.

The Asian Giant Hornet is a growing problem in the United States too. Hundreds have been found in Washington state. It has also been spotted in Canada. The hornets attack the native honeybees, called *Apis mellifera* or Western honeybee. However, these honeybees have not learned how to protect themselves from the new predators.

Scientists have been trying to work out how to protect Western honeybees from the giant hornets. This new information about poop protection could help.

Perhaps in the future, Western honeybees will find the same way of defending themselves, with poop. In the meantime, wildlife officials are trying their best to get rid of the giant hornets.

Challenge 1

1 'New scientific study shows how honeybees defend themselves' Which word is closest in meaning to 'defend'? Tick one.

Protect ☐   Attack ☐   Hold ☐

☐
1 mark

2 'It is sometimes called the "murder hornet"…' What does 'it' refer to in this sentence? Tick one.

Honeybees ☐   Bees from Vietnam ☐   The Asian Giant Hornet ☐

☐
1 mark

3 Look at the paragraph that begins 'Bees are usually clean creatures…' Find and copy one word that means 'stops someone from doing something'.

....

☐
1 mark

Challenge 2

1 According to the text, which species of honeybee has found a way of defending itself against the Asian Giant Hornet? Tick one.

Apis florea ☐   *Apis cerana* ☐   *Apis mellifera* ☐

☐
1 mark

2 '…if the hive entrance is covered with poop…' Find and copy another word from

the text that means the same as 'entrance'. ....

☐
1 mark

3 Look at the paragraph that begins 'The Asian Giant Hornet is a growing problem…' Why are the hornets a problem? Give two reasons.

a) ....

b) ....

☐
2 marks

4 Using information from the article, tick one box in each row to show whether each statement is true or false.

	True	False
Bees usually put animal poop near the entrance to their hives.		
Hornets do not like the smell of poop but they like to chew it.		
More than 300 separate bee attacks were studied.		
Giant hornets have been found all over the United States.		

☐
1 mark

Total: _____ / 8 marks

😐 **Had a go** ☐   🙂 **Getting there** ☐   😃 **Got it!** ☐

25

The Coming of the Iron Man

The Iron Man came to the top of the cliff.

How far had he walked? Nobody knows. Where did he come from? Nobody knows. How was he made? Nobody knows.

Taller than a house, the Iron Man stood at the top of the cliff, on the very brink, in the darkness.

The wind sang through his iron fingers. His great iron head, shaped like a dustbin but as big as a bedroom, slowly turned to the right, slowly turned to the left. His iron ears turned, this way, that way. He was hearing the sea. His eyes, like headlamps, glowed white, then red, then infrared, searching the sea. Never before had the Iron Man seen the sea.

He swayed in the strong wind that pressed against his back. He swayed forward, on the brink of the high cliff.

And his right foot, his enormous iron right foot, lifted – up, out into space, and the Iron Man stepped forward, off the cliff, into nothingness.

CRRRAAAASSSSSSH!

Down the cliff the Iron Man came toppling, head over heels.

CRASH!

CRASH!

CRASH!

From rock to rock, snag to snag, tumbling slowly. And as he crashed and crashed and crashed.

His iron legs fell off.

His iron arms broke off, and the hands broke off the arms.

His great iron ears fell off and his eyes fell out.

His great iron head fell off.

All the separate pieces tumbled, scattered, crashing, bumping, clanging, down on to the rocky beach far below.

A few rocks tumbled with him.

Then silence.

Only the sound of the sea, chewing away at the edge of the rocky beach, where the bits and pieces of the Iron Man lay scattered far and wide, silent and unmoving.

Only one of the iron hands, lying beside an old, sand-logged washed-up seaman's boot, waved its fingers for a minute, like a crab on its back. Then it lay still.

While the stars went on wheeling through the sky and the wind went on tugging at the grass on the cliff top and the sea went on boiling and booming.

Nobody knew the Iron Man had fallen.

Night passed.

By Ted Hughes

Challenge 1

1. Explain how the Iron Man got his name. ....

   ☐ 1 mark

2. Find and copy one word from the first part of the extract that tells you it is

   night-time. ....

   ☐ 1 mark

3. What is strange about the Iron Man's eyes? Tick one.

   They are square. ☐

   They change colour. ☐

   They turn in different directions. ☐

   ☐ 1 mark

4. '...his enormous iron right foot, lifted – up, out into space...' Find and copy one

   word in the text that means the same as 'space'. ....

   ☐ 1 mark

Challenge 2

1. Number these events from 1 to 5 to show the order in which they happen in the extract.
   One has been done for you.

His head came off.	4
His fingers waved.	
His arms came off.	
His legs came off.	
His ears fell off.	

   ☐ 1 mark

2. What sound can be heard after the Iron Man crashes onto the beach?

   ....

   ☐ 1 mark

3. 'While the stars went on wheeling through the sky and the wind went on tugging
   at the grass on the cliff top and the sea went on boiling and booming.' What does this
   sentence tell you about the effect of the Iron Man's fall on his surroundings?

   ....

   ☐ 1 mark

   Total: _____ / 7 marks

😐 **Had a go** ☐   🙂 **Getting there** ☐   😄 **Got it!** ☐

Up-Hill

Does the road wind up-hill all the way?
Yes, to the very end.
Will the day's journey take the whole long day?
From morn to night, my friend.

But is there for the night a resting-place?
A roof for when the slow dark hours begin.
May not the darkness hide it from my face?
You cannot miss that inn.

Shall I meet other wayfarers at night?
Those who have gone before.
Then must I knock, or call when just in sight?
They will not keep you standing at that door.

Shall I find comfort, travel-sore and weak?
Of labour you shall find the sum.
Will there be beds for me and all who seek?
Yea, beds for all who come.

By Christina Rossetti

Challenge 1

1 How many people are speaking in the poem? Tick one.

One person ☐   Two people ☐   Three people ☐   ☐

1 mark

2 How long will the journey take? .... ☐

1 mark

3 Reread verse 2. What is the 'resting-place'? .... ☐

1 mark

4 'Shall I meet other wayfarers at night?' What does the word 'wayfarers' mean in this question? Tick one.

Soldiers ☐   Friends ☐   Travellers ☐   ☐

1 mark

Challenge 2

1 Find and copy two words that tell you how the poet will feel at the end of the journey.

....

☐

2 marks

2 Using information from the poem, tick one box in each row to show whether each statement is true or false.

	True	False
a) The poet is on a long, hard journey.		
b) The poet is talking to a friend.		
c) The poet will have to sleep outside.		

☐

1 mark

3 'Shall I find comfort, travel-sore and weak?

Of labour you shall find the sum.'

These lines suggest that… Tick one.

the poet will have to work harder at the end of her journey. ☐

the poet will find comfort that is equal to her hard work. ☐

the poet will not find comfort at the end of her journey. ☐

☐

1 mark

Total: _____ / 8 marks

😐 **Had a go** ☐   🙂 **Getting there** ☐   😄 **Got it!** ☐

29

A Letter to Super Toys Express

RM Hodges
3 Willow Drive
Fulborough
Sussex
EN2 0BN

2 December 2021

Super Toys Express
17 Williams Drive
Southtown
LM4 9LX

Dear Sir or Madam

Re: Order number RS-Z-062273

On 22 November, I purchased the enclosed SnugglePuss toy from your website. This was a birthday gift for my nine-year-old niece Jamila. It looked like a fun toy that Jamila would enjoy and on your website it was rated four stars out of five for quality and value. This rating was based on 23 five-star reviews and eight four-star reviews from satisfied customers.

I am sorry to say that my experience with this toy is unsatisfactory.

When she opened the box, Jamila noticed immediately that only one of the SnugglePuss's ears was shaded pink. The other ear has no pink in it whatsoever. It is just green. In the picture on the website, both ears are shaded green and pink. The ears on this toy did not match.

That was the first problem. The second problem was that the SnugglePuss is supposed to sing. Well, it does not sing. It howls like a wolf! It makes the most awful sound and it scared us all to bits. I do not know of any puss that howls like a wolf. Jamila did not like the noise at all and it was a terrible let-down.

I bought the SnugglePuss toy to bring happiness, pleasure and enjoyment to my niece. On your website you say the toy is 'hilarious' and that it 'will have everyone giggling and joining in with the song'. In fact, it had quite the opposite effect. It caused great distress.

I therefore request a full refund for this item. Please note that I do not wish to receive a replacement.

I would be obliged if you would confirm receipt of this item and letter. Please also confirm that a full refund will be made within two weeks of the date of this letter.

Yours faithfully

Mr R M Hodges

Challenge 1

1 What did Mr Hodges buy for his niece? ....

1 mark

2 On the website, how many five-star reviews did the toy have? Tick one.

8 ☐   18 ☐   23 ☐

1 mark

3 What happened when Jamila opened the box? Tick one.

She noticed the ears were different colours. ☐

She noticed both ears were pink. ☐

She noticed both ears were green. ☐

1 mark

4 What was unexpected about the noise that the toy made?

....

1 mark

Challenge 2

1 'The second problem was that the SnugglePuss is supposed to sing.' What does 'supposed to' mean in this sentence?

Suggested to ☐   Meant to ☐   Pretended to ☐

1 mark

2 Find and copy one word in the letter that means the same as 'disappointment'.

....

1 mark

3 Using information from the letter, tick one box in each row to show whether each statement is true or false.

	True	False
a) Jamila is ten years old.		
b) Jamila was disappointed with her gift.		
c) Mr Hodges would like Super Toys Express to send him a new item.		

1 mark

Total: _____ / 7 marks

☺ Had a go ☐   ☺ Getting there ☐   ☺ Got it! ☐

31

Timothy Winters

Timothy Winters comes to school
With eyes as wide as a football-pool,
Ears like bombs and teeth like splinters:
A blitz of a boy is Timothy Winters.

His belly is white, his neck is dark,
And his hair is an exclamation-mark.
His clothes are enough to scare a crow
And through his britches the blue winds blow.

When teacher talks he won't hear a word
And he shoots down dead the arithmetic-bird,
He licks the pattern off his plate
And he's not even heard of the Welfare State.

Timothy Winters has bloody feet
And he lives in a house on Suez Street,
He sleeps in a sack on the kitchen floor
And they say there aren't boys like him any more.

Old Man Winters likes his beer
And his missus ran off with a bombardier,
Grandma sits in the grate with a gin
And Timothy's dosed with an aspirin.

The Welfare Worker lies awake
But the law's as tricky as a ten-foot snake,
So Timothy Winters drinks his cup
And slowly goes on growing up.

At Morning Prayers the Master helves
For children less fortunate than ourselves,
And the loudest response in the room is when
Timothy Winters roars "Amen!"

So come one angel, come on ten:
Timothy Winters says "Amen
Amen amen amen amen."
Timothy Winters, Lord.
Amen

By Charles Causley

1. Find and copy two words from the poem to complete the table.

| Timothy Winters' ears | look like | a) |
| Timothy Winters' b) | look like | splinters. |

2 marks

2. 'His clothes are enough to scare a crow…' This suggests that his clothes are… Tick one.

smart and clean. ☐

old and dirty. ☐

frightening to the other children. ☐

1 mark

3. 'And through his britches the blue winds blow.' What does the word 'blue' suggest about the winds?

....

1 mark

4. Find and copy one word in the poem that means the same as 'mathematics'.

....

1 mark

5. 'He licks the pattern off his plate…' Why does Timothy lick his plate?

....

1 mark

6. Why might Timothy's feet be 'bloody'?

....

1 mark

7. Match the statements about Timothy with the words from the poem. One has been done for you.

He is dirty	'When teacher talks he won't hear a word'
His eyes are huge	'He sleeps in a sack'
He might be deaf	'his neck is dark'
His family is poor	'his missus ran off with a bombardier'
His mum doesn't live at home	'as wide as a football-pool'

1 mark

8. Who is 'Old Man Winters'? ....

I mark

9. The poet says that the Welfare Worker 'lies awake'. Why can't the Welfare Worker sleep?

....

I mark

10. Find and copy one word that tells us how Timothy says 'Amen'. ....

I mark

11. Look at the last verse. The poet writes a prayer in this verse. Find and copy the group of words that are the prayer.

....

I mark

12. Using information from the poem, tick one box in each row to show whether each statement is true or false.

		True	False
a)	People do not think boys like Timothy exist these days.		
b)	The Welfare State can help Timothy.		
c)	The Master prays for less fortunate children.		

I mark

13. The poem describes Timothy Winters. Tick the verse that tells us about his home.

Verse I ☐

Verse 2 ☐

Verse 3 ☐

Verse 4 ☐

I mark

34

14. Number the following items from 1 to 5 to show the order in which they are mentioned in the poem. One has been done for you.

Timothy's family	
Timothy says 'Amen'	
Timothy's school lessons	3
What Timothy looks like	
Timothy goes to school	

1 mark

15. Which sentence best describes what the poem is about? Tick one.

There is nothing we can do to help poor children.

We should try to help poor children.

Poverty can have terrible effects on a child's life.

1 mark

Total: _____ / 16 marks

The Selfish Giant

'I believe the Spring has come at last,' said the Giant; and he jumped out of bed and looked out.

What did he see?

He saw a most wonderful sight. Through a little hole in the wall the children had crept in, and they were sitting in the branches of the trees. In every tree that he could see there was a little child. And the trees were so glad to have the children back again that they had covered themselves with blossoms, and were waving their arms gently above the children's heads. The birds were flying about and twittering with delight, and the flowers were looking up through the green grass and laughing. It was a lovely scene, only in one corner it was still Winter. It was the farthest corner of the garden, and in it was standing a little boy. He was so small that he could not reach up to the branches of the tree, and he was wandering all round it, crying bitterly. The poor tree was still quite covered with frost and snow, and the North Wind was blowing and roaring above it. 'Climb up! little boy,' said the Tree, and it bent its branches down as low as it could; but the little boy was too tiny.

And the Giant's heart melted as he looked out. 'How selfish I have been!' he said; 'now I know why the Spring would not come here. I will put that poor little boy on the top of the tree, and then I will knock down the wall, and my garden shall be the children's playground for ever and ever.' He was really very sorry for what he had done.

So he crept downstairs and opened the front door quite softly, and went out into the garden. But when the children saw him they were so frightened that they all ran away, and the garden became Winter again. Only the little boy did not run, for his eyes were so full of tears that he did not see the Giant coming. And the Giant stole up behind him and took him gently in his hand, and put him up into the tree. And the tree broke at once into blossom, and the birds came and sang on it, and the little boy stretched out his two arms and flung them round the Giant's neck, and kissed him.

By Oscar Wilde

Challenge 1

1. Find and copy a group of words that tell you the Giant has been waiting a long time for Spring.

   ....

2. How had the little children got into the garden? Tick one.

   Through a little hole in the wall. ☐

   Through a little door in the wall. ☐

   By climbing over the wall. ☐

3. What did the trees do when the children climbed them? Write two things.

   a) ....

   b) ....

4. Find and copy one word that shows that the children did not want to be seen or heard when they entered the garden.

   ....

Challenge 2

1. Find and copy one word that suggests the noise the birds made.

   ....

2. Where in the garden was it still winter?

   ....

3. Why didn't the little boy climb the tree? Tick one.

   He didn't want to. ☐

   He was too small. ☐

   He was too cold. ☐

4. Find and copy a word that suggests the Giant's heart became warmer.

   ....

Challenge 3

1 Why had the Giant put a wall around his garden?

....

1 mark

2 Using information from the text, tick one box in each row to show whether each statement is true or false.

		True	False
a)	The children brought Spring to the garden.		
b)	The children stayed in the garden when the Giant arrived.		
c)	The little boy ran away when the Giant approached.		

1 mark

3 How did the little boy show the Giant that he was glad to be placed in the tree? Write two things.

a) ....

b) ....

2 marks

4 From the information in the extract, what do you think will happen next?

....

....

....

1 mark

Total: _____ / 14 marks

City Jungle

Rain splinters town.

Lizard cars cruise by;
their radiators grin.

Thin headlights stare —
shop doorways keep
their mouths shut.

At the roadside
hunched houses cough.

Newspapers shuffle by,
hands in their pockets.
The gutter gargles.

A motorbike snarls;
Dustbins flinch.

Streetlights bare
their yellow teeth.
The motorway's
cat-black tongue
lashes across
the glistening back
of the tarmac night.

By Pie Corbett

Challenge 1

1. Which of these places does the poem describe? Tick one.

   A city ☐   A jungle ☐   A forest ☐

   ☐ 1 mark

2. Write the name of the animal that the poet uses to describe the cars.

   ....

   ☐ 1 mark

3. Find and copy one word that the poet uses to tell us that the headlights are acting in a human way.

   ....

   ☐ 1 mark

4. '...shop doorways keep

   their mouths shut.'

   What does the poet mean by 'their mouths'? Tick one.

   Their windows ☐   Their chimneys ☐   Their entrances ☐

   ☐ 1 mark

5. Using information from the poem, tick one box in each row to show whether each statement is true or false.

		True	False
a)	It is raining.		
b)	The city is near a motorway.		
c)	It is daytime.		

   ☐ 1 mark

Challenge 2

1. 'Newspapers shuffle by...' Which of these is closest in meaning to 'shuffle'? Tick one.

   Dance ☐

   Move quickly ☐

   Move slowly ☐

   ☐ 1 mark

2. 'Dustbins flinch.' What do the dustbins 'flinch' from?

   ....

   ☐ 1 mark

Challenge 3

1 'Streetlights bare

their yellow teeth.'

What impression does this phrase give you? Tick one:

The streetlights are friendly ☐

The streetlights are helpful ☐

The streetlights are threatening ☐

☐ 1 mark

2 '...hunched houses cough.' What does this description suggest about the houses? Write two things.

a) ....

b) ....

☐ 2 marks

3 Using information from the poem, complete the table.

Noun	Verb
radiators	**a)**
headlights	stare
b)	flinch
the gutter	**c)**

☐ 1 mark

4 Which of these statements best describes the poet's feelings about the city? Tick one.

The city is an exciting place. ☐

The city is a dangerous place. ☐

The city is a welcoming place. ☐

☐ 1 mark

Total: _____ / 12 marks

Julius Caesar

Gaius Julius Caesar is regarded as a political and military genius and is one of the most famous men to have ever lived.

Early life

He was born in Rome on 12 or 13 July 100 BCE. His father was a Roman senator. When Caesar was 16, his father died and Caesar became head of the household.

Caesar joined the army and had his first military experience when he was 19 years old. He had a very successful military career, winning the love and loyalty of his men.

Political success

Caesar returned to Rome in 78 BCE and went into government. He made powerful friends and proved himself to be an astute politician. He was made governor of Hispania Ulteria (part of modern-day Spain) when he was 38. Two years later, he was elected Consul of Rome, which was the highest political office of the Roman Republic. Two consuls were elected every year. Caesar was a great speaker and was popular with the people.

Military success

From 58 to 51 BCE, Caesar led his troops to victories throughout the province of Gaul (a large area which included modern-day France, Luxembourg, Belgium, most of Switzerland, parts of Northern Italy, the Netherlands and Germany). His success in the 'Gallic Wars' led to the expansion of the Roman Republic.

Crossing the Rubicon

Back in Rome, powerful people in the Senate were uneasy about Caesar's military success. They thought he was becoming too powerful as a military commander. They felt threatened by this. The Senate, led by Pompey who was himself a military general and a powerful politician, told Caesar that he should give up his army and return to Rome.

Caesar disobeyed the order. In 49 BCE he marched on Rome, crossing the River Rubicon in defiance of the Senate. This sparked civil war.

Dictator of Rome

Caesar did not have as many troops as Pompey but he was a brilliant military commander. After several months of war, Caesar's army was victorious at the Battle of Pharsalus in 48 BCE. Pompey was defeated.

Caesar joined forces with Cleopatra VII to secure the throne of Egypt. Caesar then made Cleopatra ruler of Egypt.

When Caesar returned to Rome, the Senate made him 'dictator for life'. Julius Caesar was then the most powerful man in the world.

Assassination

The Senate soon became anxious again that Caesar was taking too much power. For example, he ordered coins to be struck with his head on them and introduced a new calendar (called the Julian Calendar, and similar to the calendar we use today). He was also hugely popular with the citizens of Rome.

A group of Roman senators plotted to assassinate him.

On 15 March 44 BCE, Caesar was stabbed to death while he was at a meeting of the Senate. He was stabbed 23 times.

Challenge 1

1. In what year was Julius Caesar born? .... □ 1 mark

2. How old was Caesar when he had his first experience of war? .... □ 1 mark

3. Look at the section with the heading 'Political success'. Caesar 'proved himself to be an astute politician.' Which of these words is closest in meaning to 'astute' in this sentence? Tick one.

   Cruel □   Clever □   Kind □

   □ 1 mark

4. Look at the section with the heading 'Military success'. Complete the table below with one piece of evidence to support each statement.

	Evidence
It took seven years for Caesar to conquer Gaul.	
Conquering Gaul helped Rome to grow.	

   □ 2 marks

Challenge 2

1. Look at the section with the heading 'Crossing the Rubicon'. Why did the Senate call Caesar back to Rome? Tick one.

   They thought he would be more useful in Rome. □

   They wanted him to fight a different war. □

   They wanted to control his power. □

   □ 1 mark

2. Which action by Caesar marked the start of the civil war?

   ....

   □ 1 mark

3. Find and copy the name of the person who led the war against Caesar.

   ....

   □ 1 mark

4. Find and copy two words in the text that have a meaning similar to 'leader'.

   ....

   □ 2 marks

5. Look at the section with the heading 'Assassination'. 'The Senate soon became anxious again...' Find and copy another word in the text that means the same as 'anxious'.

   ....

   □ 1 mark

Challenge 3

1 Using information from the text, tick one box in each row to show whether each statement is true or false.

		True	False
a)	The Battle of Pharsalus ended the civil war.		
b)	Caesar was born in poverty.		
c)	Britain was part of Gaul.		
d)	As dictator for life, Caesar was all-powerful.		

1 mark

2 'A group of Roman senators plotted to assassinate him.' What does 'assassinate' mean in this sentence? Tick one.

Murder ☐

Strangle ☐

Stab ☐

1 mark

3 '…he ordered coins to be struck with his head on them…' What does this tell you about Caesar's character?

....

1 mark

4 Give one example from the text that shows Julius Caesar's actions had a lasting effect.

....

1 mark

5 Look at the whole text. Match each summary to the heading. One has been done for you.

Heading	Summary
Military success	Explains why the civil war began
Early life	Gives information about the Gallic wars
Crossing the Rubicon	Describes the death of Caesar
Assassination	Summarises Caesar's youth

1 mark

Total: _____ / 16 marks

😐 Had a go ☐   🙂 Getting there ☐   😃 Got it! ☐

Momotaro

'Momotaro' is a popular folktale of Japan.

One day long ago, an old woman was washing her clothes in the river when she noticed a giant peach flowing with the current. Thinking this would be a delicious treat for herself and her husband, she fished the peach out of the river and carried it home.

However, before she could cut into the peach, it burst open and a baby boy popped out. The couple were delighted. They had no children of their own and so they adopted the boy. They called him Momotaro, which means 'peach boy'.

Momotaro grew up big, strong and brave. By the time he was a teenager, he was the strongest boy in the village. The elderly couple were extremely proud of him.

One day, Momotaro came to his parents with a plan. He intended to kill the terrible demons that lived on Demon Island. These demons were much feared by the villagers, for they would often attack the village, destroying property and stealing treasure.

Momotaro's parents were not happy with this idea at first but finally he persuaded them to support his plan. They made sure that he had plenty of delicious dumplings to eat on his journey, and wished him good luck.

On his way to the island, Momotaro met a dog who asked, 'Momotaro! What have you got there?' Momotaro replied, 'I have some of the very best Japanese dumplings.' Momotaro shared a dumpling with the dog. 'Will you take me with you to Demon Island, as one of your followers?' asked the dog. 'Of course,' replied Momotaro, and the dog joined him on his journey. Later on, Momotaro met a monkey and then a pheasant. He shared dumplings with both creatures and they also decided to follow him.

After several days, they arrived at Demon Island. Each of the creatures used their own abilities and skills to fight and defeat the demons. The pheasant pecked at them. The dog bit them. The monkey scratched them. Finally, there were no demons left but the Demon Chief, who was called Akandoji.

Momotaro, being big, strong and brave, easily overpowered Akandoji. 'You have beaten me,' he said to Momotaro. 'Take all the treasure, for you have earned it!' Momotaro then gathered all the stolen treasure and, with the creatures, returned triumphantly to the village. The villagers rejoiced to see him and the old couple's joy was greater than ever to see their Momotaro again. Momotaro and his animal friends became heroes and were famous throughout the land.

With the treasure he had brought back, Momotaro and his family lived rich and peaceful lives ever after.

Challenge 1

1 Where was the old woman when she noticed the peach? .... | 1 mark |

2 '…she fished the peach out of the river…' This means that she… Tick one.

pulled the peach out. ☐

wished to pull the peach out. ☐

stole the peach. ☐

| 1 mark |

3 What popped out of the peach? .... | 1 mark |

4 Find and copy one word that tells you how the couple felt when they saw what was in the peach.

....

| 1 mark |

Challenge 2

1 The couple were childless. Find and copy the group of words that tells you this.

....

| 1 mark |

2 Why is the name Momotaro a suitable name?

....

| 1 mark |

3 Why did Momotaro decide to go to Demon Island?

....

| 1 mark |

4 What were Momotaro's parents thinking when he **first** told them his plan? Tick one.

We need to make sure he has food. ☐

This is a great idea! ☐

It's far too dangerous. ☐

| 1 mark |

5 Momotaro met three creatures on his journey. Find and copy the creatures in the order he met them.

a) .... b) .... c) ....

| 1 mark |

Challenge 3

1 'He shared dumplings with both creatures and they also decided to follow him.'
Who does 'they' refer to in this sentence?

....

1 mark

2 Find and copy one word in the text that means the same as 'abilities'.

....

1 mark

3 'Momotaro then gathered all the stolen treasure and, with the creatures, returned triumphantly to the village.' Why did they return 'triumphantly'? Tick one.

Because they had won a victory. ☐

Because they were very tired. ☐

Because they were glad to be home. ☐

1 mark

4 Which of these statements best describes the moral of this story? Tick one.

Fame and wealth will make you happy. ☐

It is better to work with others than on your own. ☐

Never take dumplings when you go on a journey. ☐

1 mark

Total: _____ / 13 marks

Loveliest of Trees

Loveliest of trees, the cherry now
Is hung with bloom along the bough,
And stands about the woodland ride
Wearing white for Eastertide.

Now, of my threescore* years and ten,
Twenty will not come again,
And take from seventy springs a score,
It only leaves me fifty more.

And since to look at things in bloom
Fifty springs are little room,
About the woodlands I will go
To see the cherry hung with snow.

*score means twenty.

By AE Housman

Challenge 1

1. In the first line, which type of tree is described as 'loveliest'? ....

2. 'Is hung with bloom along the bough…' Which word is closest in meaning to 'bloom'? Tick one.

   Leaves ☐   Branches ☐   Flowers ☐

3. 'And stands about the woodland ride…' Where does the tree stand? Tick one.

   In a small field ☐   In a small forest ☐   In a small garden ☐

4. 'Wearing white for Eastertide.' What does the word 'white' describe?

   ....

Challenge 2

1. a) In verse 1, what season is it? ....

   Give two pieces of evidence from the text that show this.

   b) ....

   c) ....

2. If 'score' means twenty, what does 'threescore' mean? Tick one.

   Twenty minus three ☐   Three multiplied by twenty ☐

   Three plus twenty ☐   Twenty divided by three ☐

3. 'Now, of my threescore years and ten…' How many years does the poet expect his life to last? Tick one.

   50 ☐   60 ☐   70 ☐

4. According to the poem, how old is the poet?

   ....

5. In verse 2, find and copy one word that suggests the poet thinks time is limited.

   ....

Challenge 3

1 'And since to look at things in bloom…' What is another word for 'since' in this line? Tick one.

Therefore ☐

After ☐

Because ☐

1 mark

2 In verse 3, find and copy a line that suggests the poet thinks time is limited.

....

1 mark

3 'To see the cherry hung with snow.' What does the word 'snow' refer to?

....

1 mark

4 In verse 3, what does the poet say he intends to do? Write two things.

a) ....

b) ....

2 marks

5 How do the poet's emotions change through verses?

....

....

1 mark

6 Which of these statements best describes the meaning of the whole poem? Tick one.

Life is limited so enjoy it as much as you can. ☐

Trees are lovely and we should protect them. ☐

No one should expect to live for ever. ☐

1 mark

Total: _____ / 18 marks

Jumbo Jet

I saw a little elephant standing in my garden,

I said 'You don't belong in here', he said 'I beg your pardon?',

I said 'This place is England, what are you doing here?',

He said 'Ah, then I must be lost' and then 'Oh dear, oh dear'.

'I should be back in Africa, on Saranghetti's Plain',

'Pray, where is the nearest station where I can catch a train?'.

He caught the bus to Finchley and then to Mincing lane,

And over the Embankment, where he got lost, again.

The police they put him in a cell, but it was far too small,

So they tied him to a lampost and he slept against the wall.

But as the policemen lay sleeping by the twinkling light of dawn,

The lampost and the wall were there, but the elephant was gone!

So if you see an elephant, in a Jumbo Jet,

You can be sure that Africa's the place he's trying to get!

By Spike Milligan

Challenge 1

1 Where was the elephant when the narrator first saw him?

_____

1 mark

2 Find and copy a group of words that tells you the narrator did not expect to find an elephant in his garden.

_____

1 mark

3 When the elephant learns he is in England, how does he feel? Give one piece of evidence from the poem to explain your answer.

How the elephant feels	Evidence

1 mark

4 The elephant says his home is 'on Saranghetti's Plain'. The correct spelling for 'Saranghetti' is 'Serengeti'. Why do you think the poet made this spelling mistake?

_____

_____

1 mark

Challenge 2

1 How did the elephant travel to Finchley? Tick one.

By train ☐

By bus ☐

On foot ☐

1 mark

2 Why did the policemen decide to tie the elephant to a lampost?

_____

1 mark

3 Draw lines to match the words about the elephant with evidence from the poem. The elephant is...

Polite   'he got lost, again.'

Homesick   'I beg your pardon?'

Confused   'I should be back in Africa'

1 mark

4 Which verse in the poem is mainly about how the elephant tried to get home? Tick one.

Verse 1 ☐

Verse 2 ☐

Verse 3 ☐

Verse 4 ☐

1 mark

Challenge 3

1 Number these events from 1 to 5 to show the order in which they happen in the poem. The first one has been done for you.

The elephant goes to sleep.	
The elephant gets to Finchley.	
The elephant disappears.	
The elephant gets to Mincing lane.	
The poet talks to the elephant.	1

1 mark

2 What were the policemen doing as dawn broke? _____

1 mark

3 'So if you see an elephant, in a Jumbo Jet…' Why is this type of plane suitable for the elephant to travel in?

_____

1 mark

4 Which of these words best describes the feeling of the whole poem? Tick one.

Humorous ☐

Serious ☐

Excited ☐

Angry ☐

1 mark

Total: _____ / 12 marks

😐 **Had a go** ☐   🙂 **Getting there** ☐   😄 **Got it!** ☐

Progress Test 2

Coming to England by **Floella Benjamin**

Floella Benjamin came to England from Trinidad in 1960. Here, she describes her experience of school in England.

It's not easy having to live and exist in two cultures at the same time, but that's what I had to get used to. At school I had to adapt to the life of an English pupil. At least that's what I was told by a teacher a couple of years after I arrived. I still had a Trinidadian accent and I liked using it because it made me feel different, someone special amongst all the other South London accents spoken in the school. So I would put it on even stronger sometimes because it was something only I could do in the class and that made me feel good. One day the teacher who took us for English asked me to read a passage from a book, so I stood up and read in my most lyrical Trinidadian accent – but in mid-flow she shouted, 'Stop, you guttersnipe. If you want to stay in my class and be understood by everyone you will learn to speak the Queen's English.'

I was devastated. I was being told to give up the one special thing I had that made me feel good about myself at school. I started to cry, not because she called me a guttersnipe – she called everyone that – but because I was being stripped of my identity in front of the class. That day I couldn't wait to get home and tell my mother what had happened. Surely I would get some sympathy from her. But Marmie, like most other West Indian parents, wanted the best education for her children. West Indians were brought up to believe that whatever the teacher said was law. School was the place where lives could be changed for the better and social standards raised. So as far as Marmie was concerned I had to abide by the rules of the teacher. After that, every morning before we left home in our immaculate school uniforms, Marmie would line us up and tell us that we were in England now, we were to go to school and learn because our passport to life was our education. We were to make sure we took advantage of every bit of knowledge that was on offer. If we did so, no one would ever be able to take it away from us.

The next time I was asked to read for my English teacher I made an attempt to speak the Queen's English. Surprisingly enough it came quite easily because I knew I had a goal, to get the best education. That was to be my reward and I wasn't going to let it slip away. I was the one who wanted the education that was on offer so I had to take charge of my destiny; if I didn't I would end up resentful. I didn't have to lose my identity either because when I got home I spoke in my natural tongue to my family. My beloved Trinidadian accent, with its rich tones, was not lost; I just had to learn to use it at the appropriate time.

1. In the first sentence, the writer uses two words that have a similar meaning.
   Find and copy the words.

   ....

   2 marks

2. '…two cultures at the same time…' Which 'two cultures' is Floella referring to?

   ....

   2 marks

3. Why did Floella like to use her accent at school? Find two reasons from the text.

   a) ....

   b) ....

   2 marks

4. At the time of this memory, how long had Floella been living in England? Tick one.

   About two years ☐

   About one year ☐

   About three years ☐

   1 mark

5. Where in England did Floella live? ....

   1 mark

6. Which of the following words best describes the teacher's reaction when Floella
   started to read? Tick one.

   Angry ☐

   Amused ☐

   Frightened ☐

   1 mark

7. Look at paragraph 1. Find and copy one name that the teacher used to refer
   to Floella.

   ....

   1 mark

8. '...you will learn to speak the Queen's English.' What did the teacher mean by 'speak the Queen's English'?

....

9. How did Floella feel when she started to cry? Find and copy one word that tells you how she was feeling.

....

10. What was Marmie thinking as Floella told her what had happened? Tick one.

The teacher was in the wrong. ☐

Floella should not have cried in class. ☐

Our culture is more important than school rules. ☐

Floella must obey school rules. ☐

11. Look at the second paragraph: '...lives could be changed for the better...' This means that lives could be... Tick one.

civilised. ☐

educated. ☐

improved. ☐

12. Look at the second paragraph. Using information from this paragraph, tick one box in each row to show whether each statement is true or false.

		True	False
a)	Marmie was a West Indian parent.		
b)	Floella thought Marmie would take her side against the teacher.		
c)	West Indian parents thought schools could raise social standards.		

13. Look at the second paragraph. Marmie believes in discipline. Which two pieces of evidence show this? Tick two.

She wanted the best for her children. ☐

She told Floella to obey the teacher's rules. ☐

She lined the children up every morning. ☐

She was a West Indian parent. ☐

2 marks

14. 'The next time I was asked to read for my English teacher...' Find and copy one group of words from this paragraph that suggests that Floella showed determination.

....

1 mark

15. This extract is from a chapter titled 'Double Identity'. Explain why 'Double Identity' is a suitable title.

....

....

....

1 mark

16. How do you think the English teacher will respond when Floella reads in class using the Queen's English?

....

1 mark

Total: _____ / 20 marks

Journey to Jo'burg

Naledi's baby sister, Dineo, is very ill. Naledi and her brother went to fetch their mother (Mma) from Jo'burg (Johannesburg) where she works. Now Naledi, Mma and Dineo are at the local hospital, waiting to see a doctor. A young woman and her baby are also in the waiting room.

All through the afternoon, they watched the patients being called one at a time by the nurse. Once the doctor himself came out. His face seemed nearly as white as his coat, except for the dark shadows under his eyes.

By mid-afternoon, Dineo needed water, but when Mma carried her to a small fountain in one corner, she almost turned away. It was so dirty! Naledi came over and struggled to cup some water in her hand without touching the sides. Then she let the water dribble over Dineo's dry little lips.

Naledi now began to feel her own empty stomach twist and turn. Her last meal had been with Grace the night before. Mma seemed to read her thoughts and sent her out to see what she could buy for a few cents. When Naledi came back with three small buns, Mma offered one to the young woman. From the way she ate it, Naledi could tell that she was very hungry too.

It was only after the light had begun to fade outside that the young woman was called to take her baby to the doctor. The child had been very quiet all afternoon, wrapped snugly against its mother's back.

In a very little time the young woman came out of the doctor's room, clutching a plastic bag. Her whole body was shaking and a man close to the door caught her just as her legs gave way.

'My baby, my baby... he's dead, he's dead!'

Her sobs filled the waiting room. Before Mma could go to comfort her, the nurse appeared calling for Dineo. The sobbing pierced Naledi's mind. She heard Mma telling her to stay where she was and she watched numbly as her little sister was now carried away. Then Naledi's gaze shifted to the plastic bag. The little baby had seemed to be sleeping so peacefully just a few minutes ago. Was it already dead then?

With head bowed, almost buried in the parcel, the woman forced herself up and stumbled out of the waiting room. Naledi's eye now fixed on the doctor's door, but instead she saw a plastic parcel being laid in a grave. It made her want to run to Mma. She sat gripping tightly on to her seat.

When Mma finally returned, her arms were empty.

'What happened, Mma?' Naledi cried.

'We must leave Dineo here and I must come back in three days... her throat is very bad... and her body is too weak...' Mma's voice sounded choked.

Before leaving Mma had to pay at the desk. There would be more to pay later, so she checked the remaining notes in her purse.

'We've nothing for bus fare... we'll just have to walk home.'

Mma looked drained.

'But it's not so far as Jo'burg, Mma!' Naledi put her arm through Mma's. She was surprised at her own sudden confidence when only a little while ago she had wanted to run to Mma for comfort herself. Well, at least they had each other.

By Beverley Naidoo

Challenge 1

1. In paragraph 1, the doctor has 'dark shadows under his eyes'. This suggests that the doctor... Tick one.

   had a lot of patients to see. ☐   hadn't had much sleep. ☐   was old. ☐   ☐

   1 mark

2. What impression does the reader get of the hospital? The table below gives three impressions of the hospital. Complete the evidence column with evidence from the text.

Impression	Evidence
Patients wait a long time.	a)
There is only one doctor.	b)
The waiting room is not hygienic.	c)

   ☐ *1 mark*

3. 'From the way she ate it, Naledi could tell that she was very hungry too.' This suggests that she ate it... Tick one.

   quickly. ☐   daintily. ☐   slowly. ☐   ☐

   1 mark

Challenge 2

1. Where was the young woman's baby while she waited to see the doctor?

   ....   ☐ *1 mark*

2. Reread the paragraph that begins 'In a very little time...' Find and copy one word in this paragraph that tells you that the young woman held the plastic bag tightly.

   ....   ☐ *1 mark*

3. What was Mma going to do to the young woman before the nurse called for Dineo?

   ....   ☐ *1 mark*

4. Reread the paragraph starting 'Her sobs filled the waiting room.' Find and copy one word that suggests Naledi showed no emotion because she was very shocked.

   ....   ☐ *1 mark*

5. 'The little baby had seemed to be sleeping so peacefully just a few minutes ago. Was it already dead then?' Which character thinks this? Tick one.

   Naledi ☐   The young woman ☐   Mma ☐   ☐

   1 mark

60

Challenge 3

1 '…but instead she saw a plastic parcel being laid in a grave.' Does Naledi really see this or not? Explain your answer.

....

1 mark

2 'Mma's voice sounded choked.' Why does she sound 'choked'? Tick one.

Because she feels emotional. ☐

Because she feels hot. ☐

Because she feels thirsty. ☐

1 mark

3 'Mma looked drained.' What does 'drained' mean in this sentence? Tick one.

Annoyed ☐

Exhausted ☐

Confident ☐

1 mark

4 What does Naledi do to comfort her mother?

....

1 mark

Total: _____ / 12 marks

The Solar System

How did it form?

Our solar system came into being around 4.5 billion years ago. It was formed from a gigantic, dense cloud of dust and gases. The cloud collapsed, possibly due to the shockwave of an exploding star (supernova). The collapsed cloud formed a nebula, which is a huge disk of spinning material.

Eventually, pressure and gravity caused the material to clump together. Some clumps smashed into each other and combined, making larger objects that became planets or moons. Some material never came together. Leftover bits and pieces of the material became asteroids, comets and meteors.

Stars and planets

Our solar system is only one of more than 500 solar systems in the Milky Way. The Milky Way is the name of the galaxy we live in. The Milky Way galaxy contains more than 200 billion stars. Only 15% of the stars in the Milky Way have planets in planetary systems.

One of those stars is the Sun. It is at the centre of the solar system and eight planets revolve around it:

Terrestrial and Jovian planets

The eight planets are divided into two categories according to their composition:

Terrestrial planets are made of rocky material.
Mercury, Venus, Earth and Mars are Terrestrial planets. They lie in the inner solar system.
They have solid surfaces. They have no rings. They have few (or no) moons. They are relatively small.

Mercury: Smallest planet. About 40% of the size of Earth.

Venus: Hottest planet. Temperature up to 465 degrees C.

Earth: The only planet we know of that can support life. This is due to its environment: it is not too close to the Sun and it has water systems.

Mars: Had a watery or icy surface 3.5 billion years ago, and may have supported life.

Jovian planets are gas planets, composed mainly of hydrogen and helium gas.

Jupiter, Saturn, Uranus and Neptune are Jovian planets. They lie in the outer solar system.

The Jovian planets are named after Jupiter.

They have gassy surfaces. They have rings. They have many moons.

They are immense in size.

Jupiter and Saturn are gas giant planets. They are mostly made up of gases, such as hydrogen and helium.

Neptune and Uranus are ice giant planets. They contain rock, ice and a mixture of water, methane and ammonia.

Jupiter: Largest planet. It has four rings. It has 79 moons.

Saturn: Second-largest planet. Its rings are so vast they would span the distance between Earth and its Moon. It has 62 moons.

Uranus: Seventh planet from the Sun. It rotates on its side and has 27 moons.

Neptune: 4.5 billion kilometres away from the Sun, and the coldest planet. It has 14 moons.

Challenge 1

1 Look at the section with the heading 'How did it form?' 'It was formed from a gigantic, dense cloud of dust and gases.' What does the word 'It' refer to? Tick one.

The Milky Way ☐   Our galaxy ☐   Our solar system ☐

1 mark

2 Number these facts from 1 to 5 to show the order in which they happened. The first one has been done for you.

An exploding star caused a shockwave.	1
Gravity and pressure pulled bits of matter together.	
A nebula was formed.	
Smaller bits of leftover matter became meteors, asteroids and comets.	
An immense cloud of dust and gases collapsed.	

1 mark

3 Reread the section with the heading 'Stars and planets'. What is our galaxy called?

_____

1 mark

4 Find and copy two words from the section 'Stars and planets' to complete the following sentence.

The Milky Way contains more than 500 **a)** _____ systems and more than 200 **b)** _____ stars.

2 marks

Challenge 2

1 The Sun is a... Tick one.

comet. ☐   star. ☐   planet. ☐

1 mark

2 Which section informs the reader how many planets are in the solar system?

_____

1 mark

3 From the diagram, which planet is...

a) Closest to the Sun? _____   **b)** Furthest from the Sun? _____

2 marks

4 Reread the section 'Terrestrial and Jovian planets'. Use the information to complete the table.

	Terrestrial planets	Jovian planets
Surface	Solid	**a)**
Rings	**b)**	Yes
Moons	Few or none	**c)**
Size	Relatively **d)**	Relatively large
Location	Inner solar system	**e)** solar system

1 mark

Challenge 3

1 Reread the information about Terrestrial planets. Find and copy a word from the text that is similar in meaning to 'conditions'.

....

1 mark

2 Using information from the text, tick one box in each row to show whether each statement is true or false.

		True	False
a)	It is possible there was life on Mars in the past.		
b)	Saturn is the coldest planet.		
c)	Jupiter has the largest number of moons.		
d)	Despite being further from the Sun, Venus is hotter than Mercury.		

1 mark

3 According to the text, where does the name Jovian planet come from?

....

1 mark

4 'Its rings are so vast they would span the distance between Earth and its Moon.' Find and copy two more words from the text that mean the same as 'vast'.

....

2 marks

5 Look at the information about Saturn. Find and copy one word that means the same as extend across.

....

1 mark

Total: _____ / 16 marks

Elfmoor Theme Park

- **Fun, thrills and excitement for the whole family!**
- **More than 60 rides and attractions**
- **An unforgettable, one-of-a-kind experience**

Thrill rides – for those who like to live on the wild side!

Spin Adventure: Loop upside down and rotate as you fly through the air. Caution: you may feel dizzy!

Air Swing: The ultimate swing experience. Suspended in mid-air, you'll get a floating feeling of weightlessness.

Log Flume: A boat ride like no other: climb then plunge down churning water chutes. Warning: you might get wet!

Cloud-Coaster: A giant catapult flings you fifty metres into the sky. Try not to scream as you come down!

Family rides – for those who like a tamer, gentler experience

Beetle Dance: Make like a bug on this much-loved rollercoaster ride.

Elves Fun Castle: Your hosts, the Elves, welcome you to their magnificent home.

Teacup Spin: A gentle roundabout ride. A cup of tea is optional!

Elfmoor Express: Meander around the park on board our very own Elfmoor Express train.

Feeling peckish?

Elfmoor Theme Park has a great range of mouth-watering, nutritious and creative options to tickle your tastebuds. Check these out!

Far Out Café – a selection of paninis, salads, sandwiches, bagels and wraps, hot and cold drinks, cakes, pastries and pies.

Go Wild Ice Cream Shop – more than 50 flavours of ice cream to choose from. Cones, sundaes and milkshakes available.

Plaice To Be – here you'll find classic fish and chips with crispy batter, fried chicken, burgers – and more.

Doughnut Palace – glazed, frosted, sprinkled or filled? Create your own doughnut masterpiece here!

Food Street – an ever-changing array of dishes from all over the globe: India, China, Korea, Indonesia, Mexico, Vietnam, Brazil...

Plan your visit

Opening times: We are open from 8 am to 11 pm, 365 days of the year.

Tickets and passes

- One-day theme park ticket (ages 9–61) £79
- Two-day theme park ticket (ages 9–61) £99
- Three-day theme park ticket (ages 9–61) £109

Special rates available for group and school visits. Contact us for information.

School Fun Days – enjoy one day at Elfmoor Theme Park. Includes free lunch.

Our other attractions

Petting Zoo – make friends with our adorable animals. We have sheep, goats, pigs, rabbits, ponies, chickens and camels.

Boating Lake – paddle your cares away as you glide across the sparkling blue lake.

Read customer reviews

Took the grandkids to Elfmoor Theme Park. They had a great time. I had a hard time trying
to get them to leave. Great family fun.

Elfmoor Theme Park is a wonderful place! We were expecting the kids to have an amazing
time but we ended up having a blast ourselves too.

I visit Elfmoor Theme Park with my mates nearly every weekend and we always have an amazing time.

Elfmoor Theme Park is a thrilling day out for the whole family!

Our promise to you

Your satisfaction is important to us and all of our services and products are 100% guaranteed. If you are not satisfied with any part of your visit to Elfmoor, please visit our Customer Service desk. If you are not 100% happy with your day at Elfmoor, we guarantee we will make it right or refund the price of your experience.

Challenge 1

1. Read the bullet points at the top of the website. Find and copy one word that means 'things that arouse someone's interest or attention'.

....

1 mark

2. Draw four lines to match the types of rides with the descriptions.

Thrill rides   Are slow, calm and easy-going
                       Are suitable for older children

Family rides   Are suitable for younger children
                       Are exciting, fast and extreme

1 mark

3. Look at the bullet points at the top of the website. Find and copy a group of words that suggests Elfmoor Theme Park offers something unique.

....

1 mark

4. Look at the section with the heading 'Thrill rides'. Find and copy another word in this section which means the same as 'Warning'.

....

1 mark

Challenge 2

1. Look at the section with the heading 'Family rides'. Which ride enables you to travel around the theme park with little effort? ....

1 mark

2. Using information from the text, tick one box in each row to show whether each statement is true or false.

	True	False
a) Elfmoor has water attractions.		
b) Elfmoor Park has exactly 60 rides and attractions.		
c) You will find llamas in the Petting Zoo.		
d) A three-day pass to Elfmoor costs £109.		
e) Elfmoor is open on Christmas Day.		

1 mark

3. Which section of the website is written to inform readers about admission prices? Write the name of the section. ....

1 mark

4. 'Elfmoor Theme Park has a great range of mouth-watering, nutritious and creative options to tickle your tastebuds.' What do the words 'mouth-watering' and 'tickle your tastebuds' suggest about the options? ....

1 mark

Challenge 3

1 Look at the section with the heading 'Feeling peckish?' The text refers to 'classic fish and chips with crispy batter'. What does the word 'classic' mean here?

High-quality ☐

Typical ☐

Traditional ☐

☐ I mark

2 Look at the section with the heading 'Read customer reviews'. Draw lines to match each customer to their review.

Grandfather — Elfmoor Theme Park is a wonderful place! We were expecting the kids to have an amazing time but we ended up having a blast ourselves too.

Parent — I visit Elfmoor Theme Park with my mates nearly every weekend and we always have an amazing time.

Teenager — Took the grandkids to Elfmoor Theme Park. They had a great time. I had a hard time trying to get them to leave. Great family fun.

☐ I mark

3 What is included if you attend a School Fun Day at Elfmoor?

....

☐ I mark

4 Look at the section with the heading 'Our promise to you'. This section is mainly about... Tick one.

What customers will do if not satisfied. ☐

Where customers can find the Customer Services desk. ☐

What Elfmoor Park promises to do if customers are not satisfied. ☐

☐ I mark

5 'If you are not 100% happy with your day at Elfmoor, we guarantee we will make it right or refund the price of your experience.' What is meant by 'refund the price of your experience'?

....

☐ I mark

Total: _____ / 13 marks

😐 **Had a go** ☐   🙂 **Getting there** ☐   😄 **Got it!** ☐

The Phoenix and the Carpet

Five brothers and sisters have found a wonderful bird called the Phoenix. This bird can speak and it wishes to visit its 'temple', a fire insurance company. The children have managed to get the Phoenix into the head office of the company.

The nice gentleman led them into a room where the chairs, and even the tables, were covered with reddish leather. He looked at the children inquiringly.

'Don't be frightened,' he said; 'tell me exactly what you want.'

'May I shut the door?' asked Cyril.

The gentleman looked surprised, but he shut the door.

'Now,' said Cyril, firmly, 'I know you'll be awfully surprised, and you'll think it's not true and we are lunatics; but we aren't, and it is. Robert's got something inside his Norfolk — that's Robert, he's my young brother. Now don't be upset and have a fit or anything sir. Of course, I know when you called your shop the "Phoenix" you never thought there was one; but there is — and Robert's got it buttoned up against his chest!'

'If it's an old curio in the form of a Phoenix, I dare say the Board —' said the nice gentleman, as Robert began to fumble with his buttons.

'It's old enough,' said Anthea, 'going by what it says, but —'

'My goodness gracious!' said the gentleman, as the Phoenix, with one last wriggle that melted into a flutter, got out of its nest in the breast of Robert and stood up on the leather-covered table.

'What an extraordinarily fine bird!' he went on. 'I don't think I ever saw one just like it.'

'I should think not,' said the Phoenix, with pardonable pride. And the gentleman jumped.

'Oh, it's been taught to speak! Some sort of parrot, perhaps?'

'I am,' said the bird, simply, 'the Head of your House, and I have come to my temple to receive your homage. I am no parrot' – its beak curved scornfully – 'I am the one and only Phoenix, and I demand the homage of my High Priest.'

'In the absence of our manager,' the gentleman began, exactly as though he were addressing a valued customer – 'in the absence of our manager, I might perhaps be able – What am I saying?' He turned pale, and passed his hand across his brow. 'My dears,' he said, 'the weather is unusually warm for the time of year, and I don't feel quite myself. Do you know, for a moment I really thought that that remarkable bird of yours had spoken and said it was the Phoenix, and, what's more, that I'd believed it.'

'So it did, sir,' said Cyril, 'and so did you.'

By Edith Nesbit

Challenge 1

1. Find and copy one word that tells you what the gentleman was like. ....

   1 mark

2. What did Cyril ask permission to do before explaining to the old gentleman what he wanted?

   ....

   1 mark

3. Who is carrying the Phoenix? Tick one.

   Cyril ☐   Robert ☐   Anthea ☐

   1 mark

4. What is the name of the fire insurance company? ....

   1 mark

5. 'If it's an old curio in the form of a Phoenix, I dare say the Board – ...' What does 'curio' mean in this sentence? Tick one.

   Old medicine ☐   Unusual object ☐   Rare bird ☐

   1 mark

Challenge 2

1. The gentleman thinks the Phoenix is some kind of bird. What kind of bird?

   ....

   1 mark

2. According to the Phoenix, why has he paid a visit? Tick one.

   To be polite ☐   To make friends ☐   To be given honour ☐

   1 mark

3. According to the Phoenix, how many phoenixes are there in existence?

   ....

   1 mark

4. How did the gentleman react when he heard what the Phoenix said?

   ....

   1 mark

5. Using information from the text, tick one box in each row to show whether each statement is true or false.

	True	False
a) Cyril and Robert are cousins.		
b) The Phoenix is old.		
c) The Phoenix thinks he is visiting a temple.		

   1 mark

72

Challenge 3

1 **a)** When the Phoenix asks to see the High Priest, who does the gentleman think he is referring to?

....

b) Give one piece of evidence from the text to support your answer.

....

2 marks

2 The gentleman thinks the Phoenix is unusual. Find and copy one word that he uses to show this.

....

1 mark

3 The Phoenix thinks himself... Which words best complete this sentence? Tick one.

less important than the gentleman. ☐

more important than the gentleman. ☐

equal to the gentleman. ☐

1 mark

4 Do you think the gentleman will help the children? Explain your answer.

....

....

1 mark

Total: _____ / 15 marks

 Had a go ☐   **Getting there** ☐   **Got it!** ☐

To Flush, My Dog (extract)

Loving friend, the gift of one,
Who, her own true faith, hath run,
Through thy lower nature;
Be my benediction said
With my hand upon thy head,
Gentle fellow-creature!

Like a lady's ringlets brown,
Flow thy silken ears adown
Either side demurely,
Of thy silver-suited breast
Shining out from all the rest
Of thy body purely.

Darkly brown thy body is,
Till the sunshine, striking this,
Alchemise its dullness, —
When the sleek curls manifold
Flash all over into gold,
With a burnished fulness.

Underneath my stroking hand,
Startled eyes of hazel bland
Kindling, growing larger, —
Up thou leapest with a spring,
Full of prank and curvetting,
Leaping like a charger.

Leap! thy broad tail waves a light;
Leap! thy slender feet are bright,
Canopied in fringes.
Leap — those tasselled ears of thine
Flicker strangely, fair and fine,
Down their golden inches.

By Elizabeth Barrett Browning

Challenge 1

1 'Loving friend, the gift of one...' Who or what is the 'Loving friend'?

....

2 What does the poet do to the dog in the first verse?

....

3 'Like a lady's ringlets brown,

Flow thy silken ears adown

Either side demurely...'

What impression do you get of the dog's ears? Give one impression.

....

4 Reread verse 3.

a) What does the poet say changes the appearance of the dog's coat?

....

b) Find and copy a word that means the same as 'change'.

....

5 Using information from verses 1 to 3, tick one box in each row to show whether each statement is true or false.

	True	False
a) The poet purchased her dog.		
b) Flush has a great variety of curls in her coat.		
c) The poet gives Flush her blessing.		

6 Find and copy a word in Verse 2 that means 'in a quiet, modest and well-behaved way'.

....

Challenge 2

1 Reread verse 4. What does the poet say happens to the dog's eyes when she strokes it? Tick one.

They change colour ☐

They get bigger ☐

They close ☐

2 The poet uses the words 'thou' and 'thy' to refer to the dog. What do these words mean? Tick one.

Them and they ☐

You and your ☐

It and its ☐

3 Look at verse 4. What colour are the dog's eyes? ....

4 Reread verse 4. A 'charger' was a horse trained for battle. Explain what the poet means by comparing the dog to a 'charger'.

....

....

5 'Full of prank and curvetting...' What does this line suggest about the way the dog moves?

....

Challenge 3

1 The poet describes different aspects of the dog. Tick the verses that are **mainly** about the dog's playfulness and energy.

Verse 1 ☐

Verse 2 ☐

Verse 3 ☐

Verse 4 ☐

Verse 5 ☐

☐ 1 mark

2 Look at verse 5. Find and copy one word that describes what the dog's ears look like.

....

☐ 1 mark

3 Look at verse 5. Find and copy one word that suggests that when it moves, the dog's ears seem to reflect the light.

....

☐ 1 mark

4 Number the following sentences from 1 to 5 to show the order in which they appear in the poem. The first one has been done for you.

The dog's ears are soft.	
It has a dark brown coat.	
Flush is gentle.	
Flush has a white chest.	
Flush is affectionate.	1

☐ 1 mark

5 'Gentle fellow-creature!' What do these words tell us about how the poet feels about her dog?

....

....

☐ 1 mark

Total: _____ / 17 marks

All About Canals

Who built the first canals?

Ancient canals The first canals were built hundreds of years ago in Egypt, Mesopotamia (modern-day Iraq and Syria), China and India. They were usually small channels built to take water from rivers to fields to grow crops. Some larger canals were built to transport cargo such as grain.

The Romans and canals In Britain, the Romans built the first canals along with roads and cities. Some people think they built the Fossdyke Navigation in Lincolnshire. It connected Lincoln, an important Roman town, to the River Trent.

Mud, weeds and potholes After the Romans left, canals silted up and became unnavigable. Roads fell into disrepair. Some bulky goods such as timber, stone and coal were transported by river. But there were big hazards such as fierce currents, low bridges and weirs.

The coming of the canals

More coal, please Much, much later, by the mid-1700s, Britain was becoming an industrial country.

As industries grew, manufacturers needed more coal to power machines, mills and furnaces. Businessmen hit on the idea of building canals to deliver coal faster.

The Duke of Bridgewater (1736–1803) The Duke of Bridgewater owned coal mines near Manchester. He gave money to build a canal to deliver coal from his coal mines to his factories.

Business booms The Bridgewater Canal was opened in 1761. It was a great success. The cost of coal halved, business boomed and lots of companies were set up to build more canals. Within 80 years, over 3500 miles of waterways linked the great ports to all the industrial areas of Britain.

Canal engineers

Building canals meant solving big engineering problems. This attracted great engineers.

James Brindley (1716–1772) James Brindley trained as a millwright. The Duke of Bridgewater heard about his reputation for inventing and fixing machinery and asked him to help plan the Bridgewater Canal.

Contour canals James' canals followed the natural contours of the land. They were easy to dig because they avoided obstacles like hills but they were long, winding and expensive to build.

The Grand Cross After the success of the Bridgewater Canal, James planned a great network of canals to connect the four main rivers of England (the Mersey, Trent, Severn and Thames) – just like motorway and train networks today. The network was called The Grand Cross because it looked like a giant cross spread over the country.

Planning and building canals attracted other clever engineers. New technology and more experience meant problems such as moving boats uphill could be solved in different ways.

William Jessop (1745–1814) William Jessop was the chief engineer of the Grand Junction Canal. He designed wide locks to take big boats. Bigger boats meant more cargo – and more money!

Thomas Telford (1757–1834) Thomas Telford was the son of a shepherd. One of his great achievements was designing Pontcysyllte Aqueduct in North Wales. It was one of the first civil engineering projects to use cast iron.

Digging the canals

Teams of navvies (short for navigators) dug the canals. Navvies used picks, spades and muscle power to dig the canals. They made them waterproof by lining them with clay and treading it down hard, or by driving cattle along the channel to trample the clay down. This is called 'puddling'.

By Canal and Rivers Trust

Challenge 1

1 According to the text, the first canals were built in Mesopotamia and three other places. Name the three other places.

....

3 marks

2 According to the text, why did canals built by the Romans become unnavigable? Tick one.

They silted up ☐   The Romans left ☐   They fell into disrepair ☐

1 mark

3 Why was it dangerous to transport goods by river? Give three of the dangers.

....

3 marks

4 Reread the section with the heading 'The coming of the canals'. Why did growing industry result in more canals being built?

....

....

1 mark

5 How do we know the Bridgewater Canal was a success? Give two examples of its success.

a) ....

b) ....

2 marks

Challenge 2

1 Reread the section with the heading 'Business booms'. Find and copy another word that is used for canals.

....

1 mark

2 'Building canals meant solving big engineering problems.' What does 'solving' mean in this sentence? Tick one.

Gluing together ☐   Finding an answer ☐   Starting ☐

1 mark

3 Reread the section with the heading 'Contour canals'. Complete the table with information from the text.

Advantage of contour canals	Disadvantages of contour canals
a) .... to dig	long, **b)** .... and **c)** .... to build

1 mark

4 Reread the section with the heading 'The Grand Cross'. Find and copy a word from the text that means the same as join.

....

I mark

Challenge 3

1 According to the text, what was one of the problems that was solved by the canal engineers?

....

I mark

2 How did William Jessop help businessmen to make more money?

....

....

I mark

3 Look at the section with the heading 'Digging the canals'. What information in the text tells us that digging the canals was hard work for the navvies?

....

I mark

4 According to the text, 'puddling' was used to... Tick one.

drive cattle.

dig canals.

waterproof canals.

I mark

5 Draw lines to match each heading to the correct summary.

Who built the first canals?   Canals built in the Industrial Revolution

The coming of the canals   Famous canals and the men who built them

Canal engineers   Canals of the ancient world

I mark

Total: _____ / 19 marks

 Had a go   **Getting there**   😃 **Got it!**

Hacker

Victoria's dad has been accused of stealing one million pounds from the bank where he works. Victoria is convinced her dad is innocent. Late one night, she decides to hack into the bank's computer to find out who really stole the money.

Gib's hair was sticking up in tufts. He'd obviously just got out of bed.

'I couldn't sleep. I came down for a glass of water,' Gib said at last. 'What're you doing?'

'None of your business,' I replied. Not for the first time I wished I could think of something devastatingly cutting and witty to say. Turning back to the PC screen, I typed in the user name and password for the third time, aware that Gib had walked over to stand behind me.

Go away, I thought sullenly.

I hated people standing behind me and watching what I was doing at the best of times. And this certainly wasn't the best of times.

ACCESS DENIED. PLEASE CONTACT SYSTEM MANAGER

I wasn't really surprised to see that message a third time.

'What're you doing?' Gib asked again.

Breathing deeply, I said, 'I'm trying to find out what's going on at Dad's bank.'

That was all the encouragement Gib needed. He almost ran to get a chair from around the dinner table before bringing it over and placing it right next to mine. He sat down. I scowled at him, but he didn't get the unsubtle hint. He didn't move. He fidgeted on his chair and looked away from me to the PC, but he didn't go away.

'So how's it going?' he asked, reading the screen.

'Not very well at the moment,' I said reluctantly. 'I've got as far as logging on to the bank's network but I haven't managed to log on to Dad's account to do anything yet. And I've tried three times.'

'So why can't you log on?' Gib asked.

'I ... I think they must've disabled Dad's account. I couldn't have got the password wrong three times in a row.'

'Can't you double-check what password you *did* type in, then?' asked Gib.

I shook my head. 'When you type in a password, it doesn't show on the screen. Passwords are supposed to be secret. They wouldn't be very secret if anyone walking past your screen could see your password every time you logged on.'

'So what're you going to do now?'

'Why the sudden interest?' I couldn't help asking.

There was a pause before Gib answered.

'I want to find out what's going on just as much as you do. I want to help too,' Gib said, looking down at the carpet.

Yeah, but when I try to help, you call it crawling, I thought.

All of a sudden my eyes were stinging again. I took a deep breath and opened my eyes wide, and the stinging faded. When I was sure I wouldn't embarrass myself, I said, 'I'll log on to the computer using Dad's second account – his TEST account. He uses it for checking and testing programs. Let's hope this works.'

This time I clicked on the TEST LOGON icon.

Enter username: TEST

Enter password:

'Cross your fingers,' I said to Gib. My hands hovered over the keyboard. Please let this work, I thought desperately. If this didn't work then I'd be stuck.

I typed in the password – JABBERWOCKY44. The screen cleared. Then:

UNIVERSAL BANK DEVELOPMENT SYSTEM

THIS SYSTEM IS FOR THE EXCLUSIVE USE OF UNIVERSAL BANK PERSONNEL. ANY UNAUTHORIZED ACCESS TO THIS ACCOUNT MAY LEAD TO PROSECUTION.

You have 3 new mail messages

test>

appeared on the screen.

'Yeah! I'm in!' I yelled, before I remembered that Mum was upstairs.

'Shush!' Gib said urgently.

By Malorie Blackman

Challenge 1

1 'He'd obviously just got out of bed.' Which word is closest in meaning to 'obviously' in this sentence? Tick one.

Plainly ☐   Quietly ☐   Secretly ☐

☐

1 mark

2 Why did Gib come downstairs? Give two reasons.

a) ....

b) ....

☐

2 marks

3 Was Victoria happy that Gib had come downstairs? Give one piece of evidence from the text to explain your answer.

....

☐

1 mark

4 Before Gib arrived, how many times had Victoria typed the user name and password?

....

☐

1 mark

Challenge 2

1 Gib was keen to understand what Victoria was doing. What did he do that shows this?

....

☐

1 mark

2 What did Victoria do to try to make Gib go away? ....

☐

1 mark

3 '"Not very well at the moment," I said reluctantly.' What does 'reluctantly' mean? Tick one.

Angrily ☐   Sadly ☐   Unwillingly ☐

☐

1 mark

4 Victoria failed to log on to her Dad's account three times. What conclusion does she draw from this?

....

☐

1 mark

5 'Yeah, but when I try to help, you call it crawling, I thought.' What does 'crawling' mean in this sentence? Tick one.

Moving on your hands and knees ☐

Trying to get approval from someone ☐

Feeling sorry for yourself ☐

☐

1 mark

84

Challenge 3

1 'When I was sure I wouldn't embarrass myself...' What did Victoria almost do that might have caused her embarrassment?

....

1 mark

2 'My hands hovered over the keyboard.'

   a)   What does 'hovered' suggest about Victoria's hands?

        ....

   b)   What does this suggest about how Victoria was feeling?

        ....

2 marks

3 Why did Gib tell Victoria to 'Shush!'? Give two reasons

   a) ....

   b) ....

2 marks

4 Number the following events from 1 to 5 to show the order in which they happened. The first one has been done for you.

For the third time, Victoria gets the message ACCESS DENIED.	
Gib says he wants to help Victoria.	
Victoria wishes Gib would go away.	
Victoria logs on to the TEST account.	
Gib comes downstairs and finds Victoria.	1

1 mark

Total: _____ / 16 marks

 Had a go    **Getting there**   **Got it!**

Progress Test 3

Extract from

A *Christmas Carol* by Charles Dickens

Once upon a time – of all the good days in the year, on Christmas Eve – old Scrooge sat busy in his counting-house. It was cold, bleak, biting weather: foggy withal: and he could hear the people in the court outside, go wheezing up and down, beating their hands upon their breasts, and stamping their feet upon the pavement stones to warm them. The City clocks had only just gone three, but it was quite dark already – it had not been light all day: and candles were flaring in the windows of the neighbouring offices, like ruddy smears upon the palpable brown air. The fog came pouring in at every chink and keyhole, and was so dense without, that, although the court was of the narrowest, the houses opposite were mere phantoms. To see the dingy cloud come drooping down, obscuring everything, one might have thought that Nature lived hard by, and was brewing on a large scale.

The door of Scrooge's counting-house was open that he might keep his eye upon his clerk, who in a dismal little cell beyond, a sort of tank, was copying letters. Scrooge had a very small fire, but the clerk's fire was so very much smaller that it looked like one coal. But he couldn't replenish it, for Scrooge kept the coal-box in his own room; and so surely as the clerk came in with the shovel, the master predicted that it would be necessary for them to part. Wherefore the clerk put on his white comforter, and tried to warm himself at the candle; in which effort, not being a man of strong imagination, he failed.

'A merry Christmas, uncle! God save you!' cried a cheerful voice. It was the voice of Scrooge's nephew, who came upon him so quickly that this was the first intimation he had of his approach.

'Bah!' said Scrooge. 'Humbug!'

He had so heated himself with rapid walking in the fog and frost, this nephew of Scrooge's, that he was all in a glow; his face was ruddy and handsome; his eyes sparkled, and his breath smoked again.

'Christmas a humbug, uncle!' said Scrooge's nephew. 'You don't mean that, I am sure?'

'I do,' said Scrooge. 'Merry Christmas! What right have you to be merry? What reason have you to be merry? You're poor enough.'

'Come, then,' returned the nephew gaily. 'What right have you to be dismal? What reason have you to be morose? You're rich enough.'

Scrooge, having no better answer ready on the spur of the moment, said, 'Bah!' again; and followed it up with 'Humbug!'

'Don't be cross, uncle!' said the nephew.

'What else can I be,' returned the uncle, 'when I live in such a world of fools as this? Merry Christmas! Out upon merry Christmas! What's Christmas time to you but a time for paying bills without money; a time for finding yourself a year older, but not an hour richer; a time for balancing your books, and having every item in 'em through a round dozen of months presented dead against you? If I could work my will,' said Scrooge indignantly, 'every idiot who goes about with "Merry Christmas" on his lips should be boiled with his own pudding, and buried with a stake of holly through his heart. He should!'

'Uncle!' pleaded the nephew.

'Nephew!' returned the uncle, sternly, 'keep Christmas in your own way, and let me keep it in mine.'

'Keep it!' repeated Scrooge's nephew. 'But you don't keep it.'

'Let me leave it alone, then,' said Scrooge. 'Much good may it do you! Much good it has ever done you!'

1. According to the text, what day of the year was it? ....

| 1 mark

2. Where did Scrooge work? ....

| 1 mark

3. What time of day was it? ....

| 1 mark

4. '…it had not been light all day…' Why had it not been light all day?

....

| 1 mark

5. Find and copy a group of words that tells us the atmosphere was thick and dirty.

....

| 1 mark

6. '…the houses opposite were mere phantoms.' What is another word for 'phantoms'? Tick one.

Ghosts ☐   Outlines ☐   Shapes ☐

| 1 mark

7. '…Nature lived <u>hard by</u>, and was <u>brewing</u> on a large scale.' Choose the best words to match the text above. Circle both of your choices.

…Nature was [close by / far away / solid] and was [breaking / squeezing / producing] lots of fog.

| 1 mark

8. Why did Scrooge keep the door of his counting-house open?

....

1 mark

9. '…in a dismal little cell beyond, a sort of tank…' What impression do you get of the room where the clerk worked? Give two impressions.

a) ....

b) ....

2 marks

10. 'But he couldn't replenish it…' Who or what does 'he' refer to in this sentence?

....

1 mark

11. How did the clerk try to keep warm? Find two things.

a) ....

b) ....

2 marks

12. '"Bah!" said Scrooge. "Humbug!"' What does 'humbug' mean? Tick one.

Nonsense ☐   Perhaps ☐   Correct ☐

1 mark

13. 'What right have you to be dismal?' Find another place where the writer uses the word 'dismal' to describe something. What was it?

....

1 mark

14. 'What reason have you to be morose?' 'Morose' means… Tick one.

cold. ☐   gloomy. ☐   cheerful. ☐

1 mark

15. What impressions do you get of Scrooge's nephew? Give one impression, supporting your answer with evidence from the text.

....

....

2 marks

16. Using information from the text, tick one box in each row to show whether each statement is true or false.

		True	False
a)	Scrooge owns the counting-house.		
b)	Scrooge is poor.		
c)	Scrooge dislikes Christmas.		
d)	Scrooge is generous.		

1 mark

17. "'What else can I be," returned the uncle, "when I live in such a world of fools as this?'"
Find and copy another word in Scrooge's speech that means the same as 'fool'.

....

1 mark

18. How would you describe the feeling of the whole extract? (For example, is it mostly humorous, or sad, or something else?) Give a reason for your answer, based on the text.

....

....

2 marks

19. Based on the whole text, how likely is it that Scrooge's nephew will persuade his uncle to celebrate Christmas?

....

1 mark

20. 'Out upon Merry Christmas!'

a) From this speech, give two things that Scrooge has against Christmas.

   1 ....

   2 ....

b) What does this tell us about Scrooge's attitude towards life?

....

....

3 marks

Total: _____ / 26 marks

89

Pages 6–13 Starter Test

1. Jumped out of the window [1] 2. Extremely [1]
3. the Eiffel Tower [1] 4. very quickly [1] 5. a) True,
b) True, c) False [1] 6. The vet [1] 7. in Streaker's
bottom [1] 8. two-legs [1] 9. Being able to get away [1]
10. Because Trevor Two-Legs wants to persuade
Streaker that the vaccination will prevent her getting
diseases that could make her very ill. [1] 11. *Starship* [1]
12. California [1] 13. reusable [1] 14. a) False, b) True,
c) True [1] 15. Moon, Mars [2] 16. challenges [1]

17.

Mars 3 landed on Mars.	2
SpaceX was founded.	4
Eugene Cernan walked on the Moon.	3
Starship was announced by SpaceX.	5
'Buzz' Aldrin walked on the Moon.	1

[1]

18. so that people can live there [1]
19. land people on Mars [1]
20. it will probably not be successful [1]
21. the flu [1]
22. can be passed from one person to another [1]
23. its worth/it can 'travel right around the earth' [1]
24. If you feel like smiling, do it. [1]
25. Because a smile is passed from one person to
    another (is 'infectious'), over time it could be
    passed to ('infect') everyone in the world. [1]

Pages 14–15

Challenge 1

1. ruling themselves [1] 2. a ruler [1] 3. simple,
foolish [2] 4. a log [1]

Challenge 2

1. They thought he was boring. [1] 2. He sent a Crane
to be king of Frogland, knowing that the Crane would eat
the Frogs. [1] 3. Sad [1] 4. a) True, b) False, c) False [1]

Pages 16–17

Challenge 1

1. accidental [1] 2. Quarrelled [1] 3. they hated one
another [1]

Challenge 2

1. upset [1]
2. the brother [1]
3. 'I was in the wrong.' [1]
4. Because he admitted he was in the wrong and by
   doing this he ended the quarrel, which was the
   right thing to do. [1]

Pages 18–19

Challenge 1

1. Two answers from: German Toast, Eggy Bread,
   French Fried Bread, Nun's Toast, pain perdu/lost
   bread [2]
2. lost bread [1]
3. a) False, b) True, c) True, d) False [1]
4. 15 minutes [1]

Challenge 2

1. Ingredients → Food items you need
   Equipment → Tools you need
   Method → What you need to do [1]
2. to taste [1] 3. Whip [1] 4. Serving suggestions [1]

Pages 20–21

Challenge 1

1. London [1] 2. They were scared [1] 3. 'in the army
far away' [1] 4. Mythical [1] 5. Beast [1]

Challenge 2

1. a) True, b) False, c) False [1]
2. His dad puts drawings for Lenny in his letters. [1]
3. It would have been difficult for post to be collected
   on a daily basis/regularly where Dad was fighting
   so several letters would be sent together. [1]
4. The Robinsons' house has been destroyed/
   bombed. Evidence: the house 'wasn't there any
   more' / their things 'were lying all over the street
   amongst the rubble and broken glass' [2]

Pages 22–23

Challenge 1

1. darling [1]
2. In the dirt [1]
3. coal [1]
4. Biting → around on the rug
   Rolling → for clams in the yard
   Chewing → buttons off a shirt
   Digging → the roots of a rose
   Finding → a lost silver mine [1]

Challenge 2

1. Warrior [1]
2. blackberries and ice cream [2]
3. That the adult doesn't have fun / doesn't enjoy life
   anymore / is too old to have fun. [1]

Pages 24–25

Challenge 1

1. Protect [1] 2. The Asian Giant Hornet [1]
3. deters [1]

Challenge 2

1. *Apis cerana* [1] 2. mouth [1]
3. a) The hornets attack native / Western honeybees.
   b) These honeybees do not know how to / have not learned how to defend themselves. [2]
4. a) False, b) False, c) True, d) False [1]

Pages 26–27

Challenge 1

1. He is made of iron. [1] 2. darkness [1] 3. They change colour. [1] 4. nothingness [1]

Challenge 2

1.

His head came off.	4
His fingers waved.	5
His arms came off.	2
His legs came off.	1
His ears fell off.	3

[1]

2. the sound of the sea [1] 3. The Iron Man's fall has no effect on his surroundings. [1]

Pages 28–29

Challenge 1

1. Two people [1] 2. from morn to night / all day [1]
3. an inn [1] 4. Travellers [1]

Challenge 2

1. travel-sore, weak [2]
2. a) True, b) True, c) False [1]
3. the poet will find comfort that is equal to her hard work [1]

Pages 30–31

Challenge 1

1. a SnugglePuss toy [1] 2. 23 [1] 3. She noticed the ears were different colours. [1] 4. It howled like a wolf. [1]

Challenge 2

1. Meant to [1]
2. let-down [1]
3. a) False, b) True, c) False [1]

Pages 32–35 Progress Test 1

1. a) bombs b) teeth [2] 2. old and dirty [1] 3. they are cold / icy [1] 4. arithmetic [1] 5. because he is hungry [1]

6. because he is so poor, he doesn't have any shoes [1]

7.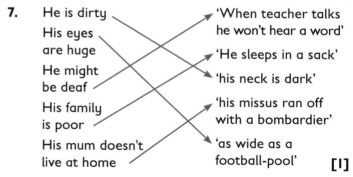

8. Mr Winters / Timothy's dad [1]
9. The Welfare Worker is worried about Timothy. [1]
10. roars [1]
11. 'Timothy Winters, Lord. Amen' [1]
12. a) True, b) False, c) True [1]
13. Verse 4 [1]
14.

Timothy's family	4
Timothy says 'Amen'	5
Timothy's school lessons	3
What Timothy looks like	2
Timothy goes to school	1

[1]

15. Poverty can have terrible effects on a child's life. [1]

Pages 36–38

Challenge 1

1. at last [1] 2. Through a little hole in the wall. [1]
3. a) covered themselves with blossoms / blossomed;
b) waved their arms (branches) [2] 4. crept [1]

Challenge 2

1. twittering [1] 2. in one corner / in the farthest corner [1] 3. He was too small [1] 4. melted [1]

Challenge 3

1. To keep the children out. [1]
2. a) True, b) False, c) False [1]
3. a) he threw his arms around the Giant's neck / hugged the Giant; b) he kissed the Giant. [2]
4. Child's own answer, e.g. the Giant will knock down the wall; children will play in his garden forever; it will always be Spring. [1]

Challenge 1

1. A city [1] 2. lizard [1] 3. stare [1] 4. Their entrances [1] 5. a) True, b) True, c) False [1]

Challenge 2

1. Move slowly [1]
2. the sound of the motorbike [1]

Challenge 3

1. The streetlights are threatening [1]
2. Suggested answers: a) 'hunched' suggests the houses are crouched over. Some children may suggest the houses are trying to protect themselves / trying to stay dry in the rain. b) 'cough' suggests that the houses are ill / not healthy. [2]
3. a) grin, b) dustbins, c) gargles [1]
4. The city is a dangerous place. [1]

Challenge 1

1. 100 BCE [1] 2. 19 [1] 3. Clever [1]

4.

	Evidence
It took seven years for Caesar to conquer Gaul.	'From 58 to 51 BCE, Caesar led his troops to victories throughout the province of Gaul…'
Conquering Gaul helped Rome to grow.	'His success in the "Gallic Wars" led to the expansion of the Roman Republic.'

[2]

Challenge 2

1. They wanted to control his power. [1]
2. crossing the River Rubicon [1]
3. Pompey [1]
4. Any two from: dictator, commander, ruler [2]
5. uneasy [1]

Challenge 3

1. a) True, b) False, c) False, d) True [1]
2. Murder [1]
3. That he was egotistical/proud/had a sense of his own self-importance. [1]
4. He introduced the Julian calendar that is similar to the calendar we use today. [1]

5.

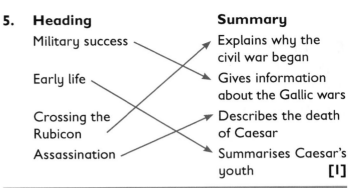

Heading	Summary
Military success	Explains why the civil war began
Early life	Gives information about the Gallic wars
Crossing the Rubicon	Describes the death of Caesar
Assassination	Summarises Caesar's youth [1]

(Military success → Gives information about the Gallic wars; Early life → Summarises Caesar's youth; Crossing the Rubicon → Explains why the civil war began; Assassination → Describes the death of Caesar)

Challenge 1

1. in/at the river [1]
2. pulled the peach out [1]
3. a baby boy [1]
4. delighted [1]

Challenge 2

1. 'They had no children of their own' [1] 2. because it means 'peach boy' and the boy came from a peach [1] 3. to kill the demons [1] 4. It's far too dangerous. [1] 5. a) dog, b) monkey, c) pheasant [1]

Challenge 3

1. both creatures / the monkey and the pheasant [1]
2. skills [1] 3. Because they had won a victory. [1]
4. It is better to work with others than on your own. [1]

Challenge 1

1. the cherry (tree) [1] 2. Flowers [1] 3. In a small forest [1] 4. the tree's flowers/blossom [1]

Challenge 2

1. a) Spring, b) the cherry tree is in bloom, c) it is Eastertide [3] 2. Three multiplied by twenty [1] 3. 70 [1] 4. twenty (also accept 20) [1] 5. only [1]

Challenge 3

1. Because [1] 2. 'Fifty springs are little room' [1]
3. white cherry blossom [1] 4. a) walk around the woodland, b) enjoy seeing the cherry trees in flower / bloom [2]
5. In verse 1, he feels delight when he sees the cherry blossom; in verse 2, he feels sad because the reality is that life is limited; in verse 3 he feels grateful/glad to be alive to enjoy the blossom, knowing that time is limited. [1]
6. Life is limited so enjoy it as much as you can. [1]

Challenge 1

1. in the narrator's garden [1]
2. 'You don't belong in here' [1]
3.

How the elephant feels	Evidence
Accept any feeling words similar to: worried, upset, concerned, dismayed.	He says, 'Oh dear, oh dear'.

[1]

4. Answers may mention: for comic effect / humour; because the poet is unfamiliar with the place name and / or the correct spelling for the place; because the elephant pronounced it as 'Saranghetti' and the poet wrote it as he heard it. Other plausible explanations should be awarded a mark (e.g. the narrator could be a child). [1]

Challenge 2

1. By bus [1] 2. Because the elephant was too big to fit into a cell / because the cell was too small for the elephant to fit into. [1]

3. Polite — 'he got lost, again.'
   Homesick — 'I beg your pardon?'
   Confused — 'I should be back in Africa' [1]

4. Verse 2 [1]

Challenge 3

1.

The elephant goes to sleep.	4
The elephant gets to Finchley.	2
The elephant disappears.	5
The elephant gets to Mincing lane.	3
The poet talks to the elephant.	1

[1]

2. sleeping [1]
3. 'Jumbo' means very large; a jumbo jet is a very large plane so the elephant will fit into it. [1]
4. Humorous [1]

Pages 54–57 Progress Test 2

1. live and exist [2] 2. English, Trinidadian [2] 3. a) it made her feel different/special b) it made her feel good [2] 4. About two years [1] 5. South London [1] 6. Angry [1] 7. guttersnipe [1] 8. speak with an English accent [1] 9. devastated [1] 10. Floella must obey school rules. [1] 11. improved [1] 12. a) True, b) True, c) True [1] 13. She told Floella to obey the teacher's rules. She lined the children up every morning. [2]

14. One from: I had a goal / I wasn't going to let it slip away / I had to take charge [1]

15. Answers should refer to: living in 'two cultures at the same time'; retaining her Trinidadian identity at home and learning to use her 'natural tongue' at the 'appropriate time'. [1]

16. Children should predict that the teacher will be pleased with Floella. [1]

Challenge 1

1. hadn't had much sleep [1] 2. a) they waited 'all through the afternoon' b) 'the doctor himself came out' c) the water fountain 'was so dirty!' [1] 3. quickly [1]

Challenge 2

1. wrapped against her back / holding onto her back [1]
2. clutching [1]
3. comfort her [1]
4. numbly [1]
5. Naledi [1]

Challenge 3

1. No. Naledi imagines this, because she is in shock. [1] 2. Because she feels emotional. [1] 3. Exhausted [1] 4. she puts her arm through her mother's arm / she links arms with her mother [1]

Challenge 1

1. Our solar system [1]
2.

An exploding star caused a shockwave.	1
Gravity and pressure pulled bits of matter together.	4
A nebula was formed.	3
Smaller bits of leftover matter became meteors, asteroids and comets.	5
An immense cloud of dust and gases collapsed.	2

[1]

3. the Milky Way [1] 4. a) solar, b) billion [2]

Challenge 2

1. star [1] 2. Stars and planets [1] 3. a) Mercury, b) Neptune [2] 4. a) Gassy, b) No, c) Many, d) small, e) Outer [1]

Challenge 3

1. environment [1] 2. a) True, b) False, c) True, d) True [1] 3. Jupiter [1] 4. Any two from: gigantic, immense, giant, huge [2] 5. span [1]

Challenge 1

1. attractions [1]

2.

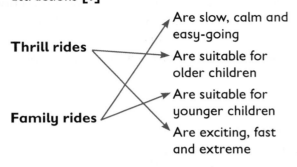

Thrill rides → Are suitable for older children

Thrill rides → Are exciting, fast and extreme

Family rides → Are slow, calm and easy-going

Family rides → Are suitable for younger children

[1]

3. one-of-a-kind [1] 4. Caution [1]

Challenge 2

1. Elfmoor Express [1] 2. a) True, b) False, c) False, d) True, e) True [1] 3. Plan your visit [1] 4. that the options are delicious / taste good [1]

Challenge 3

1. Traditional [1]

2.

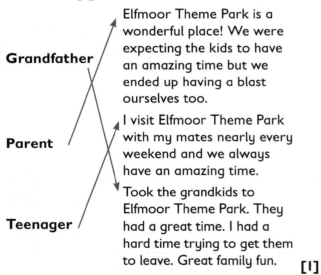

Grandfather → Took the grandkids to Elfmoor Theme Park. They had a great time. I had a hard time trying to get them to leave. Great family fun.

Parent → Elfmoor Theme Park is a wonderful place! We were expecting the kids to have an amazing time but we ended up having a blast ourselves too.

Teenager → I visit Elfmoor Theme Park with my mates nearly every weekend and we always have an amazing time.

[1]

3. free lunch [1] 4. What Elfmoor Park promises to do if customers are not satisfied. [1] 5. repay the money paid for the tickets [1]

Challenge 1

1. nice [1] 2. shut the door [1] 3. Robert [1]
4. Phoenix [1] 5. Unusual object [1]

Challenge 2

1. a parrot [1] 2. To be given honour [1] 3. one [1]
4. He turned pale / passed his hand across his brow. [1]
5. a) False, b) True, c) True [1]

Challenge 3

1. a) the manager of the insurance company
   b) 'In the absence of our manager,' the gentleman began [2]

2. 'remarkable' [1]

3. more important than the gentleman [1]

4. Accept either yes or no as long as a suitable explanation is given, e.g. Yes because he is nice, he wants to help, and he believes the children. No because he doesn't really believe the Phoenix can speak / he will think he is dreaming. [1]

Challenge 1

1. the author's dog, Flush [1] 2. she puts her hand on the dog's head / she gives the dog a benediction [1]
3. Any of the following impressions: they are soft, shiny and delicate, like a lady's ringlets, or like silk. [1]
4. a) sunshine, b) alchemise [2] 5. a) False, b) True, c) True [1] 6. demurely [1]

Challenge 2

1. They get bigger [1] 2. You and your [1] 3. hazel [1]
4. She means that the way the dog moves shows it is strong, excited and full of expectant energy, like a charger getting ready for battle. [1] 5. That the dog energetically prances around in a showy manner. [1]

Challenge 3

1. Verse 4 and Verse 5 [1] 2. tasselled [1] 3. Flicker [1]

4.

The dog's ears are soft.	3
It has a dark brown coat.	5
Flush is gentle.	2
Flush has a white chest.	4
Flush is affectionate.	1

[1]

5. That the poet loves / feels great affection for her dog, that she admires its gentleness ('gentle'), and that for her the dog is on a par with humans (it is a 'fellow creature'). [1]

Challenge 1

1. Egypt, China and India [3]

2. They silted up [1]

3. fierce currents, low bridges, weirs [3]

4. Industry needed more coal and it was quicker to deliver it by canal. [1]

5. Two from: price of coal halved; business boomed; more companies were set up to build more canals. [2]

Challenge 2

1. waterways [1] 2. Finding an answer [1] 3. a) easy, b) winding, c) expensive [1] 4. 'connect' [1]

Challenge 3

1. moving boats uphill [1]
2. He designed wider locks, which could take bigger boats with more cargo. This made each boat trip more profitable. [1]
3. the fact that they had to use muscle power [1]
4. waterproof canals [1]
5.

Who built the first canals?	Canals built in the Industrial Revolution
The coming of the canals	Famous canals and the men who built them
Canal engineers	Canals of the ancient world [1]

Pages 82–85

Challenge 1

1. Plainly [1] 2. a) he couldn't sleep, b) he wanted a glass of water / he was thirsty [1] 3. No. She wants him to go away: 'Go away, I thought sullenly.' [1] 4. twice [1]

Challenge 2

1. He quickly ('almost ran') fetched a chair and sat beside her. [1] 2. scowled at him [1] 3. Unwillingly [1] 4. that the bank must have disabled his account [1] 5. Trying to get approval from someone [1]

Challenge 3

1. she almost started to cry / burst into tears [1]
2. a) That her hands were hanging in the air without moving. b) That she was feeling nervous. [2]
3. a) Because he wanted Victoria to be quiet. / Because noise / yelling might wake up Mum, who was asleep upstairs. / b) Because he didn't want Mum to find out what they were doing. / Because he wanted to keep what they were doing secret from Mum. [2]
4.

For the third time, Victoria gets the message ACCESS DENIED.	3
Gib says he wants to help Victoria.	4
Victoria wishes Gib would go away.	2
Victoria logs on to the TEST account.	5
Gib comes downstairs and finds Victoria.	1

[1]

Pages 86–89 Progress Test 3

1. 24 December / Christmas Eve [1]
2. in a counting-house [1]
3. 3 pm [1]
4. because it was foggy [1]
5. 'palpable brown air' [1]
6. Ghosts [1]
7. close by, producing [1]
8. to keep watch over his clerk / to check his clerk was working [1]
9. Two answers from: it was small and basic, almost like a prison ('little cell'); it was gloomy and depressing ('dismal'); it was like a cage or something you keep animals or reptiles in ('tank') [2]
10. the clerk [1]
11. a) he puts on a comforter (scarf), b) he tries to warm himself with the candle [2]
12. Nonsense [1]
13. the clerk's room [1]
14. gloomy [1]
15. One answer from: he is cheerful ('cheerful voice', 'gaily'); he is warm-hearted (he wishes his uncle a merry Christmas); he is energetic (he walks quickly); he is good-humoured (he asks his uncle what there is to be sad about and pokes gentle fun at him) [2]
16. a) True, b) False, c) True, d) False
17. idiot [1]
18. Answers will vary. Accept any answer that is plausible based on the text. For example, it could be described as humorous, because Scrooge is portrayed as an exaggerated character for comic effect; or depressing, because of the descriptions of the darkness and the fog; or sad, because Scrooge is mean-spirited and hates Christmas, and his clerk is cold and the counting-house is dismal. [2]
19. Extremely unlikely [1]
20. a) Any two from: people go into debt at Christmas; Christmas is when people realise they are one year older but no wealthier; Christmas is when people do their yearly accounts and realise they have lost money.
    b) It suggests that Scrooge thinks there is nothing more to life than money. [3]

Fill in your score for each progress test in the window of the rocket.

Progress
Test 1

Progress
Test 2

Progress
Test 3